All My Love, Gib

A Soldier's Letters to his Wife, 1942–1944

edited by
Kaaren Andersen Nowicki

The scanned images of Gib's letter, dated January 13, 1943, found on pages 22 to 25 are courtesy of the Center for American War Letters Archives, Leatherby Libraries at Chapman University.

ISBN: 978-1-959563-46-4

Maudlin Pond Press
P.O. Box 53
Tybee Island, GA 31328
www.maudlinpond.com

Printed in the United States of America

Editors' Note

Creating this book was a labor of love for Kaaren Andersen Nowicki. Her father's letters to her mother from December 1, 1942, to November 23, 1944, had fired her imagination since childhood. Kaaren, like her father, was quite a writer, in 2016 publishing *Spiritual Triage*, a book inspired by her work as a chaplain at Atlanta's Crawford Long Hospital. Two years later she turned her attention to her father's letters, choosing 127 of the 300 he wrote home from his U.S. Army postings in the U.S. and abroad, and transcribing the excerpts included here. Alas, on February 22, 2024, before she was able to finish her final edit, she lost her life to cancer.

With the assent of Kaaren's family, her writing group, Inkfingers – comprising Riki and Paul Bolster, Deborah Miller, Kate Ravin and Carla Schissel – finished the editing process. We have lightly edited Kaaren's text and Gib's letters for clarity and consistency, changing the grammar and punctuation as little as possible. In accordance with standard editorial practice, an ellipsis (. . .) appears where Kaaren has chosen to omit words or sentences from the letters. We have made educated guesses in the rare places where information was unavailable, or her intent was unclear.

Introduction

One rainy fall weekend, I sat at my mother's knee-hole desk, playing school. It was 1949, and I had just turned seven. My imaginary pupils had produced a pile of arithmetic tests, and I needed a red pencil to correct their work. I found it in the top drawer, finished my task, returned the pencil to its slot, and, feeling curious, decided to investigate the contents of the other drawers. I fingered a bottle of ink, a checkbook, my kindergarten report card, a handful of paperclips

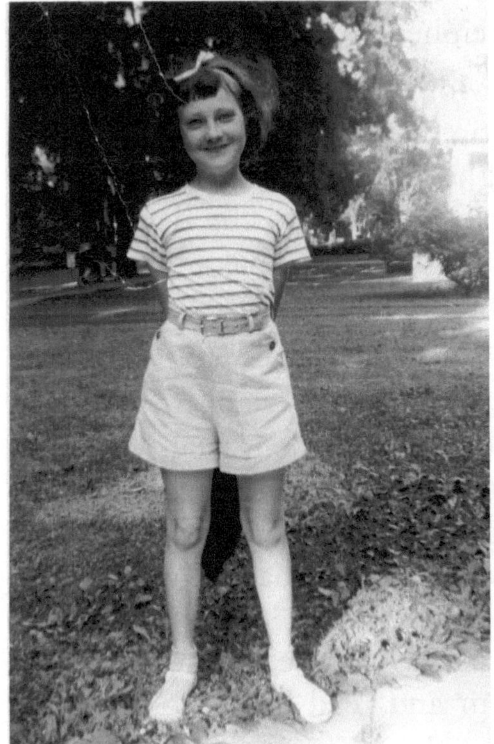

and some important-looking documents in an impressive folder. These items were all interesting enough, but what came to light in the big bottom-right-hand drawer took my breath away: a glittering silver-and-blue box certain to contain something of great value.

My mother arrived on the scene to help me pry the big shiny package from the drawer. We untied the white velvet ribbon and opened the hinged lid to discover a huge collection of old letters. I'd expected something more exciting, like a ballerina doll or new black patent leather party shoes. Instead, I saw hundreds of envelopes, each of them edged with red-and-blue chevrons and hand addressed in black ink. My disappointment dissolved when Mom let me know that the letters, grouped into bunches tied with blue satin ribbons, were written by my father during World War II. My family had helped me understand that he died in a forest in Germany when I was two years old. I didn't remember my father, but the photograph in our bookcase proved I had known him: a familiar-looking soldier standing on my grandmother's front porch holding a blond toddler – me. My seven-year-old brain somehow recognized that the hands holding me in that photograph had written these letters and that he was still with us in written form. My mom said I could look at the (more than 300) letters and touch them carefully, and that I could begin to read them when, as a third grader, I had conquered the skill of deciphering cursive writing.

The letters stayed in Mom's bottom desk drawer for years, and I read them from time to time, soaking up aspects of my dad's personality. I laughed at his puns, appreciated his gift of storytelling and grew to understand the depth of his homesickness. I appreciated his ability to make new friends and explore new places. I got to know the young Harold Gilbert Andersen, and as I did so, I also was able to mourn my loss.

When my mom moved to a retirement facility, the letters moved to our house and became a presence in our family's life. They make appearances after family dinners and come to picnics at the lake. They've joined us on road trips, and they make good reading on winter nights when it feels best to stay home by the fireplace. Our usual practice is for each of us to pull out a letter at random and read it to the group. In this way, my father, forever young, maintains a place in our lives. We know about his basic training and his time in Officer Candidate School. We know about the friends he met, the adventures they shared, the importance of letters from home, his love for his wife and baby and the value of a well-tailored GI coat. We know about the challenges of trigonometry and the excitement of shipping out for Europe. We witness Gib's attempt to stay positive for his reader's sake even as he begins to fully understand the danger of his situation.

The silver box has collapsed, the satin ribbons have frayed, but the letters maintain a prominent place in my office under the eaves. It has been seventy-three years since my snooping brought them to light, and now it is time to share my treasure with anyone interested in the World War II experiences of a young American soldier from Whitewater, Wisconsin, as told in letters to his wife.

Poppy & Karen

Part One

Basic Training

December 1, 1942-March 11, 1943

December 1, 1942, Milwaukee to Fort Sheridan, Illinois

Dearest, I can still smell your perfume from this morning when you took me to the station. I'll never wash this shirt. Got to Milwaukee about 9:30, walked to the induction station and whizzed right through all my business there by 10:30. Sat around and waited until I and about 200 other men went out to dinner together. We walked about a mile each way for tough liver and slightly burnt onions. Back at the induction center nothing much happened until 4:00 when we walked another mile and back for supper. Came back to induction center, were sworn in and left shortly thereafter for Chicago and Fort Sheridan via the North Shore Line. We've been issued barracks bags, toilet articles, mess kit, canteen, gloves and handkerchiefs. Kiss the baby.

All my love, Gib

(Fort Sheridan, built in 1887 along Lake Michigan just north of Chicago, was a U.S. Army post in operation until 1984. An Army Reserve base continues to use 90 acres. The remaining property, about 500 acres, is divided between a golf course and a variety of ongoing commercial and residential development. An outdoor museum honors the fort's past.)

December 2, 1942, Fort Sheridan

Dearest, they woke us at 5:30 for chow and then issued uniforms. I now have two pairs of woolen pants and two khaki wool shirts and two khaki cotton shirts, plus all sorts of stuff to fill two barracks bags. Nothing has happened since then, but tonight we get the Articles of War read to us and receive a lecture on military courtesy. Meals are OK, and I'm getting along fine. Don't write to me here because I won't be here long enough to get mail. But when I get to the next camp (wherever it is), you can write me every day and also send me some wire coat hangers. They gave us uniforms, but nothing to hang them on. Kiss Kaaren.

All my love and XXX, Gib

(A picture of my dad as a child shows a gangly, grinning boy with one knee in a dented coaster wagon. He may have had a dirty face and rumpled hair, but his crisp white shirt was neatly buttoned and tucked into his well-fitting shorts. The grandson of a tailor, he appreciated quality fabrics, a good fit and appropriate grooming. These interests continued in his army career. Never completely satisfied with the tailoring of his GI overcoat, he visited several alteration shops during his two years of service.)

Later, December 2, 1942, Fort Sheridan

Dearest, we got things accomplished this afternoon. We made out War Bond deductions, allotment forms and got our typhoid and smallpox shots. Tonight, they'll read the Articles of War to us. After that we get our GI haircuts, and then there's nothing more to do around here except wait to be shipped out for basic training. I'm sending some stuff home for you to take care of. Please put the three papers in our lock box. Send certified copies of Kaaren's birth certificate to the address on the little mimeographed slip of paper along with a certified copy of our marriage certificate. This is necessary to start the allotment checks coming your way. Must go to hear A. of W. read to us.

All my love and XXX to you both, Gib

December 3, 1942, Fort Sheridan

Dear Baby, you should see my haircut . . . even too short for me. I was there twenty minutes, and there were six men ahead of me in that chair, so figure it out. We each spent about three minutes in the chair. Once around with the clippers, cut the top, shave the neck and out of the chair. Rumor has it we'll be shipped out tonight, but who can tell? It's deadly boring just waiting for things to happen. To cheer myself up, I look at your pictures. I am so tired tonight. We get up so early in the morning that I long for the good old days when I didn't have to get up until 6:00 to get the baby. When I get to be a general, I will have a davenport in my tent and sleep until noon.

Love to both of you, Gib

December 10, 1942, traveling from Fort Sheridan, Illinois, to Camp Callan, California

Dearest, I'm writing on a train from somewhere in California. The camp we're headed to is near San Diego. That's all I know so far. We left the Dearborn Station in Chicago Monday night on the Santa Fe route and have been on that road all the way. Our train has about fifteen cars filled with soldiers and sailors on shipment orders. Sometimes the train stops at a Fred Harvey for a meal and sometimes we eat in the dining car. When we stop, we get into formation and march to meals. It was snowy, cloudy and cold all the way through Kansas and for the last two days we've been going through mountains and desert. Not many signs of civilization. We play cards and read magazines for amusement. We sleep in upper and lower berths. Porter is now on the way to make up the berths for the night so I must buzz off. We were due in camp this afternoon but are behind schedule so that means an extra night on the train and camp early in the morning.

All my love and XXX to you and Kaaren and Granny

(Granny was Gib's mother, known as Lil, Ma or Lanny. Grammy was my mother's mom, also known as Gert or Gertie. They were the gold standard of grandmotherhood. They were fun and funny and kind and often helped my mom care for me. I was also blessed with aunts: Moonie, Ginny, Cille and Joan, who were also fun and funny and kind and often available for babysitting stints.)

December 12, 1942, Camp Callan, California

Dearest, this will be a short letter because of time, so vital information first. Address: Pvt. H. G. Andersen, Jr. 36287040, Battery D, 57th AA Tv. Bn., Camp Callan, California. Please send me some wire coat hangers – ten or more if you can get that many. See if you can find a spiral notebook about the right size for taking notes. They hold a guy up around here for that kind of stuff – hangers are ten cents apiece. This camp is about fifteen miles north of San Diego and 125 miles south of Los Angeles. Got here about noon today, and we're at work getting settled in. Now I must shower, shave and get to bed early. I love you and miss you so much. This army wouldn't be so bad if privates could sleep with their wives.

Love and XXX to you and Baby, Gib

December 14, 1942, Camp Callan, California

Dearest, Sunday is a day of rest even in the army. We can lie in bed until seven o'clock and then get up and eat a hearty breakfast of pancakes and sausages. I went to church this morning. I guess the sermon was enlightening, but I didn't hear much of it. Too many thoughts of my own – about Christmas and how it will be to spend it away from home and family. But I guess we are fighting for the right to be with our families in future Christmases, and it is better to miss a few now than to miss them all in the future. Speaking of Christmas, I was going to have my picture taken in time to send home before the 24th, but I have to wait for all the buttons for my blouse to arrive so I can sew them on for the photographer. I wish I'd taken my camera to basic training, but probably couldn't use it much here at camp due to security. There are all kinds of secret equipment lying around on the coastline and from my barracks window I can see the ocean just about half a mile away. It would be easy for a sub to sneak in here and shell the place, so we have black-out, or rather dim-out every night and the streetlights have shields on the seaward side. There are very few lights at night, and if someone is out after lights out at 9:00, it would be easy for them to walk into the wrong barracks and become pretty confused. Tomorrow I am barracks guard which means I will have to stay around the barracks all morning to see that no strangers walk in here and steal stuff. We might get to see a movie tonight: "White Cargo," with Hedy Lamarr and Walter Pidgeon. The double feature last night was so bad we could see the corn growing out of the screen.

All my love and XXX, Gib

December 16, 1942, Camp Callan, California

Dearest, it begins to look as if this is going to be one hell of a tough place. We've been going on the double from 7:30 a.m. to 7:30 p.m. We drill on a parade ground three blocks south of the barracks, and we go to lectures and movies in a building a mile north of the barracks. This whole battalion consists of men who are potential officer candidates, and there are about 1,300 of us. The powers that be expect a lot out of us, and they mean to get it. We get hollered at for the slightest iniquity. We were issued rifles after chow tonight, and that is just one more thing to worry about. It has to be cleaned and oiled every day, and we must memorize the serial number. In spite of all my griping, I'm glad I'm here because it's a good opportunity to get somewhere. Our platoon sergeant and corporal are two fine fellows, but they are so overworked that they don't have time to be nice and say "please" and "thank you." I love you and I miss you so much.

Kiss baby, and here are some kisses for you. XXX, Gib

(I thought Gib would have been familiar with a shotgun because I'd always heard that he and Barbara, his Springer Spaniel, liked to go squirrel hunting in the woods outside of town. His brother, my Uncle Jimmy, was a golfer, not a hunter. Once I asked Uncle Jimmy if my dad liked to play golf, too. He said Gib would play a round or two to be sociable, but what he really liked was taking long walks in the woods with his dog. Jimmy claimed Gib took a gun along just as a prop. He proved his theory by pointing out that man and dog always came home smiling and relaxed but never with a bag of squirrels.)

December 17, 1942, Camp Callan, California

Dearest, your letter and Lil's both came today, and they cheered me up no end. I was on KP today. From 5:30 in the morning until 7:30 at night. Steady grind all the time. Woke up this morning when someone got me up for KP. I asked him what time it was, and he said, "What the Hell do you care? Get up." You've got to have a sense of humor to get along in this place. You also have to look good. Every time we step out of the barracks we must be fully dressed, with neckties and caps. Tomorrow I will have been in the camp for a week. Seems like a year. Lights out now.

Love and XXX to you and Kaaren, Gib

December 18, 1942, Camp Callan, California

Dearest Genie, tonight we learned how to fold a raincoat and how to put a pack on. Also learned how to adjust slings on rifles to aim. I am so glad I had the State Guard and ROTC training because most of this stuff is only a review. I hope to get more letters from you soon. Mail call is after evening chow and is the most popular hour of the day. Good night, now.

All my love, Gib

December 20, 1942, Camp Callan, California

Dearest Mommy, busy all day with drill, lectures, formations and then right after evening chow, we started cleaning the barracks and our personal effects to get ready for morning inspection. We cleaned up until lights out and then got up at 5:00 a.m. to start cleaning some more. Roll call at 6:10, when we had to be outside fully dressed. Inspection was from 7:30 to10:30. Then we drilled and had instructions until chow. This afternoon we started our personal interviews with the battery commander, so, my name beginning with "A," I go first. I didn't have the slightest idea what to do in front of the commander, so I kept asking questions, so he didn't have time to ask me any, and we got along fine. We have the rest of the afternoon off, so I'll write Pa today, too. Your Dec. 17 letter arrived today. Please tell me more about Kaaren. I wish I could watch her grow. Hurry those pictures.

All my love and kisses, Gib

(Gib called his parents Ma and Pa. Pa had been a young officer in WWI and now in WWII he was a Colonel in charge of an army supply facility in Australia. I don't think he made it home until after the war was over in 1945. My handsome Uncle Jimmy was also in the army, but he never received orders to ship to Europe.)

December 23, 1942, Camp Callan, California

Dearest Genie, what a day–got two letters and a package from you and packages from the O'Connors and Winklemans. Your Christmas package is very lovely, and everything in it is so nice. I appreciate it so much. I am sorry I can't send you anything for Christmas, but you know the situation. All I can send is my eternal love. I'm glad to hear about Mrs. Leffingwell's sister because there's a slight possibility we might get passes for Christmas Day, and it would be nice to know someone to look up in San Diego. As I said before, we are only about twenty miles from there. Today we had instructions on 50-caliber machine guns, and we had a lecture on airplane identification. I've already eaten a lot of your cookies, and the boys in my corner of the barracks are happy to help with that. Red Skelton is on the radio. Makes me homesick for the times we would go upstairs to our room on Tuesday nights to listen to the radio in bed. I'm in bed now, but you're not here to scratch my back. All my love to you and Baby. Let us hope and pray we won't be separated for many more Christmases.

Love and XXX and thanks for the swell package, Gib

(The O'Connors, Winklemans and Leffingwells were all family friends. The Leffingwells had a men's clothing shop in the same space where Gib's grandfather once had his tailoring shop. Mr. O'Connor worked at the bank with my grandfather. The Winklemans had invited Barbara, the springer spaniel, to live with them while Gib was away. Later letters reveal that Barbara had different plans.)

December 24, 1942, Camp Callan, California

Darling Genie, I had some more 50-cal.-machine-gun instruction this afternoon. I should be able to strip that thing blindfolded pretty soon. Also, more bayonet drill today. I hope I never get into a spot where I have to use a bayonet. We also had an "alert" today. When they spring an alert, everybody drops everything, gets into sidearms, gas mask and helmet. Those not assigned to gun crews double-time it down into the gullies around here and hide in the brush. Those on gun crews man their guns. Lots can happen around here. Please don't bawl me out any more for not writing every day because I do write every day I get a chance. If I don't write, it's because I'm too busy, and I probably will be too busy once in a while. We have to learn in three months what usually takes four years to teach. They are shoving it at us pretty damn fast. I know how much my letters mean to you, and I say again, I'll write every time I get a chance. I love you so and miss you so. Those letters are something that I do to keep up the morale of us both. I get just as much out of writing them as you do receiving them. Lecture concluded. Now I'm going to shower and shave before lights out. Mornings come early and I like to avoid the rush in the shower room. G'night now.

Kisses to you and Kaaren, from Gib

Christmas Day, 1942, Camp Callan, California

Dearest Genie, this is just about the dullest Christmas Day I have known. I got up too late for breakfast, so I've been feasting on the cookies and candy you made for me. We had a good Christmas dinner this afternoon, and then we swept, scrubbed and mopped the barracks, getting ready for tomorrow's inspection. We are on the second floor, and there is a little ledge running around the building, and there I was, running around like a squirrel. No stepping back to admire my work. The gale-force wind made it even more fun. I may be able to get to San Diego or La Jolla to get the strap on my Christmas watch shortened. I've got a bridge game lined up tonight with Noyes and two others, so I'll have something to occupy my mind. I'd tell you how much I miss you, but I find it too hard to talk about that today. I'm glad we got to have a phone conversation. Good night, Dear.

All my love to you both, Gib

(If Gib had been back in Whitewater, he would have experienced Christmas at his childhood home on Center Street. He would have seen the Christmas tree standing in the corner of the living room, and he would have smelled the rib roast cooking in the kitchen. My mom and I would have been there, too, along with Lady Barbara, the dog. My grandpa, known to me as Colonel, would have picked out some records for background music. I think we would have heard a medley of show tunes, Christmas music and some marches played by the Fifth Army Band. Uncle Jimmy loved to play parlor games, so after a dessert of meringue shells filled with ice cream and hot fudge, we would have played one of his favorites before we exchanged presents.)

December 26, 1942, Camp Callan, California

Dearest Genie, we have barracks and ranks inspection every Saturday, but tomorrow we'll go back into the hills someplace, pitch tents, tear them down and march back again. Maybe there will be a machine gun crew alert, too. If so, we have to go to the supply room, get out a machine gun and all the stuff that goes with it, take it about two miles to a placement and set it up. Then we tear it down again and take it back to the supply room. I'm going to bed now. Five-thirty comes early.

All my love, Gib

December 31, 1942, Camp Callan, California

Dearest, Corp. Wolfe of our platoon is now back from furlough, and yesterday afternoon he took us on a run through the ravines going down to the beach. In my whole life I was never so completely out of gas as I was when we got through. Speaking of furlough, I know for sure I'll get one after we finish Officer Candidate School (OCS).

All my love to the best wife in the world. . . yes, you. Gib

January 5, 1943, Camp Callan, California

Darling Genie . . . Sometime will you send me my best-looking pair of brown shoes? We can wear them after 5:00, and it would feel so good to get out of my G.I. clunkers. Please tell Lil that my new Christmas watch is swell. I have to get into town to have the band shortened because if I wear it now, it falls so far up my arm that I have to undress to find out what time it is. We're now getting all the finishing touches for our uniforms. We have pretty buttons for our jackets and bright red braid for our caps.

All my love and kisses to the best two girls in the world. Gib

January 6, 1943, Camp Callan, California

Dearest, I got the nicest letter from you today. It had lipstick prints all over it. Thank you. Your letters are what keep me going around here. This letter gave me enough energy to take Uncle Otto's Christmas check to the local Bank of America branch. I told the man at the window that I used to be a banker, and we had a little chat about the racket. There was a line of other customers behind me waiting to transact their business. I didn't realize the branch closed in three minutes, but when I did, we cut our conversation short, and I got out of the way. I'll go earlier next time so we can finish our conversation. Lights out now, so must quit.

All my love, Gib

January 7, 1943, Camp Callan, California

Dearest Baby, one of the men who came from Sheridan with us got his discharge today. He is over 38, and it was rough for him, so he decided to get out. Mickey Butler is his name. From Cascade, Wisconsin. I hate to see him go because he is a grand fellow. It makes me wonder how many of these men I meet in the army and make friends with I'll see after the war. One of them is sitting right next to me right now. Harvey Heck from Milwaukee. Managed to qualify for my marksmanship badge today on the range. Going to bed now. 5:30 comes pretty fast around here. I love you always. Hurry up and send me some pictures of yourself and Kaaren.

Love and XXX, Gib

January 8, 1943, Camp Callan, California

Dearest Genie, if I ever get a furlough before going to O.C.S. I will come home and spend all the time with you. We will sleep until lunch. Later we'll dress leisurely and have a hot meal. We'll go to the movies and sit in the back and cuddle up. The next day, we'll take Kaaren for a walk, and I'll push the buggy. I love you so very much I am glad they keep me so busy, so I won't have time to think of how awful it is to be away from you. All my love to the best girls in the world: Genie and Kaaren.

All my love, Gib

January 12, 1943, Camp Callan, California

Darling Genie . . . we went on an eight-mile-hike to-day along the cliffs and through the scrub brush. We walked through some mighty beautiful country, too . . . the bluffs along the coast with big pines growing on them. We could see way back inland. We got within three miles of Del Mar, where Bing Crosby lives, but saw nothing of him. We went about a quarter of a mile through deep sand, which was pretty tough, but our platoon made it through the whole exercise with no injuries. I'm the platoon leader in tomorrow's parade, so I better get some rest.

All my love, Gib

January 13, 1943, Camp Callan, California

My darling Baby, your letters are what I look forward to every day. They keep me going. I love you and miss you so much. When you have time, will you send me that picture I took of you last spring? The one where you are sitting on the banister of the side porch and your pretty knees are shyly peeking out under your skirt. I would like to have that here with me. After math class tonight, I went to the service club and ate a whole pint of chocolate ice cream all by myself.

All my love, Gib

My Darling Baby -   Tuesday
    Now 8:30. Went to Math class
at 6:00 tonite, & afterwords went
over to the service club & ate a whole
pint of chocolate ice cream by myself.
Not as good as good old Luick's, but
it was good. Math classes are very
strange here. They give you a bunch
of mimeographed lessons, & every
man for himself. Work as fast or
slow as you please. From 6 to 8
every nite Monday thru Thursday.
The class is about a mile from here,
so I don't go often. Get most of my
work out of the books you sent.
    Got no letter from you tonite, but
one from Pa. If some of us don't
go to mail call, some one else usually
gets all the mail for the platoon,
but maybe some one missed up
on one of my letters. If so, I

22

get it tomorrow. We had the parade today in which I was a ~~battery~~ platoon leader. It was the best parade I've been in, but maybe I'm prejudiced. The captain said it was pretty good, too. So I ain't the only one.

I'm beginning to get a good tan on my face & neck, & also on the backs of my hands.

Today was pretty dull on the instruction stuff. Mostly going over what we have already had. On the way back from the hike yesterday saw something I forgot to tell that was interesting. Big French 155 mm. cannons. Could tell they were French guns, because the directions on the gun were in French. Seacoast guns.

Today we were asked how many didn't know how to swim.

I was tempted to raise my hand, just to get in some swimming, but I didn't. You never can tell about deals like that. Chances are pretty good that I would have to march a long ways on Saturday afternoons to go to those lessons. When some one gets xcited about anything around here, we tell them to "Keep a cool stool". Just another army phrase thought you might be interested in. We have some other quainter ones, but I won't tell them to you. Too vile. I'm worrying about my language when I get out of this place. Have to think what I am saying.

By the way, have you started again yet?
Find out about the State & Fed.
Income tax, & let me know, & I will
figure out the dope for you as close
as I can. I don't think we have to
pay one anyway, because of exemption
being more than my salary.
Goodnight now, & all my love &
kisses to my little lover.

K.C.

January 15, 1943, Camp Callan, California

Dearest Genie . . . Mrs. Kenyon (Mrs. Leffingwell's sister) is coming up to camp for me tomorrow. She'll take me to her house in San Diego for Sunday dinner. It will be nice to be with a family and eat off something other than Army dinnerware for a change. I had K.P. today. We dressed chickens all afternoon. About two dozen of them. If we have chicken at the Kenyon's, I think I'll pass out. Write and tell me more about Kaaren. I miss you both so much. I wish she'd learn to write so she could send me letters, too. It's your letters that keep me going.

All my love, Gib

January 16, 1943, Camp Callan, California

Darling Baby, went to dinner at the Kenyons finally and had a very nice time. We had fried chicken, peas, potatoes, and all that sort of stuff. It was wonderful to eat quietly and comfortably around a family table. But it did make me lonesome for you. I kept thinking about how nice it would be if you and Kaaren were there, too. Kaaren would have had fun playing with the Kenyons' granddaughter, who is 13 months old. I played with the baby for a while. She was cute but not as cute as ours. The Kenyons' son is an ensign in the Naval Air Corps, and he was there today, too.

All my love, Gib

January 18, 1943, Camp Callan, California

Dearest, we climbed a nice big hill behind La Jolla this afternoon and could see all the way into Mexico to the south. San Diego was just below us. Lots to see here, and of course hitchhiking is against the regulations. Still, there's nothing to prevent a uniformed man from standing at the edge of a highway with an expectant look on his face. Got my watch strap shortened today at a shop in La Jolla. Now I go to bed and dream of you. I'll take your most recent letter to tuck under my pillow. It still smells just like the hair behind your ears where you dab perfume.

All my love, Gib

January 20, 1943, Camp Callan, California

Dearest One . . . three of us in this platoon get on the same details all the time: Andersen Bramwell and Bassin. We've been on K.P. and table-waiter duty together twice so far and also on the gun crew. We work as a team and really do produce. There are some mighty fine fellows here. Kiss the baby for me.

All my love, Gib

January 21, 1943, Camp Callan, California

Darling Genie, do you think the Winklemans want to get rid of Barbara, or do you think maybe it's Barbara's own decision to take up residence with your mom and sisters? She never spent much time with the Winklemans, but she knows your family so well. She's always enjoyed their company, and they like her, too. They don't even mind if she sits on the couch. You write that as soon as the Winklemans let her out each morning she goes around the corner, crosses Main Street, gets up on the porch and looks longingly in your mom's living room window. Of course, they invite her in, and she spends the day. They send her back in the evening, and she goes obediently, but reluctantly, returning each morning. Do you think your mom would mind having Barbara live with her until I come home? I know she'd be safe and happy there. I'm so mad that I can't get home to take care of things like this. Barbara is such a good dog. I'd hate to lose her. I love you, darling, and I long for the day when I can be back home with you and Kaaren and Barbara, too.

All my love, Gib

(Barbara lived at the house of Grammy (my maternal grandmother) for the rest of her life. She was pampered and petted and loved by all, including my Uncle Clarence, who taught her the finer points of deer- and duck-hunting. It was fun for me to be with Barbara because I knew she'd been Gib's dog in her earlier days. My mom wasn't a dog person, so she was out of the loop when it came to Barbara's care. I think Gib's mom, Lanny, would have taken her in, but Barbara seemed to have made her own choice.)

January 24, 1943, Camp Callan, California

Darling, when I was in San Diego today, I got a bottle of colorless fingernail polish to cover my brass buttons so they won't tarnish. If we get paid tomorrow, I'm going to town and buy a khaki shirt. The three shirts issued to me look as if they'd fit Oliver Hardy. I thought they'd shrink in the laundry, but no such luck. Have I told you how we have to make up our bunks in the morning? The mattress must be folded double, blankets, sheets and comforter folded and placed on top of the mattress. Foot lockers must also be put on the bunks as well as shoes and slippers. Clothes must be hung up and <u>buttoned</u>. Not sure how this practice leads to excellent soldiering, but it's a must-do. Must close now and get to bed and dream of you.

Good night, my love. Gib

PS. I've sent your mom a sincere letter of thanks for giving Barbara a home. What a relief!

January 26, 1943, Camp Callan, California

Dearest Mommy, what a war this is. K.P. all day and tomorrow morning until school time. This noon I went with the food truck out to feed the battery. It took us an hour-and-a-half to find them. They had hiked two hours to get to the spot. Before that, they'd gone through the obstacle course several times. At first, I was glad to be on K.P., but now I sort of wish I'd had the experience. It was a different kind of experience on the food truck. I got gravy on my shoes from all the splashing around on the bumpy ride. Now I have to study logs and algebra before lights out. And clean the gravy off my shoes. You are my whole life, and I ain't fooling.

XXX, Gib

January 27, 1943, Camp Callan, California

Darling Genie . . . we have a sort of fraternal organization here in this platoon and have meetings every night. The purpose of the club is to have a common meeting place and time to gripe about the day's events. I am treasurer of this organization. No dues, no initiation fees, no fines. Anyone who can gripe in colorful, flowing language is eligible for membership. It is silly, but we're all getting stir-crazy. Good night now.

I love you dearly, Gib

January 28, 1943, Camp Callan, California

Darling Genie, your letters mean everything. The photos are wonderful, too. That's a good picture of Kaaren. I showed it off to everybody in the platoon until they absolutely refused to look at it anymore. Somebody saw your picture tonight and wondered how such an 8-ball like me ever got such a beautiful girl to marry him. I sort of wonder that, too . . . It's been dreary and cloudy all day. The natives tell me this is the rainy season, and it will rain for weeks at a time. If you were here, we could spend Sunday afternoon taking a nap and listening to the rain fall on the roof. Now I go to bed to dream of you.

All my love, Gib

January 31, 1943, Camp Callan, California

Darling Baby, I have a few minutes to recline on my bunk and rest for a while. I'm thinking of all the good times and the lovely life we've had together so far. I'm also thinking about what fun we'll have living together after this is over. We are two lucky people to be so happily in love with each other and to have a daughter as beautiful as her mother. You are doing all the parenting right now. When I come home, I will go into father mode, and we will live together like a family should. Resting time is over now. We're off on a gas mask drill.

All my love, Gib

February 4, 1943, Camp Callan, California

Darling, I forgot to tell you my troubles on table-waiting detail yesterday. I was putting away some clean dishes, and they were in a dishpan which I had sitting on a stepladder. The dishpan fell to the floor and six gravy bowls broke to pieces. Luckily, the sergeant wasn't around. The cook told me to make the pieces disappear real quick before the sergeant came back. I did just that, and no one but the cook and I are the wiser. Must get to bed, but first, one more thing. You don't have to ask if you can spend money on some new clothes. That money is yours, too, you know, so go ahead and buy that satin blouse.

All my love, Gib

February 7, 1943, Camp Callan, California

Dearest, I was Battalion Messenger yesterday, and it was fun. I rode all over camp on a bicycle delivering documents, forms, papers and such to various officers on the post. When my legs got tired, I rode around on the bus. Tomorrow I'm going to church in La Jolla with a bunch of the Catholic boys. There isn't a Lutheran Church there, so I'll just tag along with them.

All my love, Gib

(Gib's family attended the Congregational Church. He joined the Lutheran Church after he married my mother. I benefited by attending both churches when I was growing up. I liked the liturgy and ritual of the Lutheran Church and enjoyed the spirited organ music, the flute solos and interpretive dance team of the Congregational Church. Both churches had excellent holiday events featuring craft sales and delicious buffet luncheons.)

February 8, 1943, Camp Callan, California

Dearest Genie, I guess this is my valentine to you. Roses are red, sweet peas are pink, you're a honey, that's what I think. I love you so much it hurts. Without you and baby Kaaren to fight for, I wouldn't be worth anything here. I'm fighting so I can come home and live in peace with my family for the rest of my life. I was remembering our wedding and how afraid I was that I wouldn't be able to keep you happy and contented; but so far, I guess I have. How about it? If you were here now, I'd kiss you so good that your toes would curl. I thank God that you are my wife . . . I went to town this morning with those boys I was telling you about. We got there at 9:00, an hour early for mass, so we bummed around for an hour and then went in. It's a beautiful Spanish mission-type church with white plaster and oak beams on the inside. After church, we looked in the shop windows for a while and then found a place for dinner. There were five of us in the group, and two others from the platoon sat with us at dinner, so we had quite a party. I had lobster, which wasn't as good as the lobster that you and I had at the Heidelberg in Madison last year. Those were the good old days. After dinner we went down to the beach and played in the sand like a bunch of school kids. Good night, my valentine.

I love you, Gib

February 10, 1943, Camp Callan, California

Darling Genie, we took a hike this afternoon carrying our full field equipment: blanket, shelter tent, mess kit, toilet articles, change of underwear, clean handkerchief, canteen and cup. The first half hour was the hardest, and then we got used to it. Nobody fell out today. The captain moved the second platoon out in front today because we were all singing, and he wanted to hear the music. This morning, I appeared for an interview before the O.C.S. Board and tomorrow at 1300 I go to the hospital for a physical examination. Must close and take my bath now. I smell like a dead fox.

All my love, Gib

(As I understand it, Gib's basic training at Camp Callan was the first step in being accepted for enrollment in O.C.S. He had enlisted in hopes of that, thinking his experience as an officer might be of benefit when it came time to find interesting work when the war was over. Probably he could have returned to the bank, but maybe he wanted to keep his options open.)

February 12, 1943, Camp Callan, California

My Darling, today I was a beach guard. I had to perch on a little ledge halfway down the cliff with a telephone back to the range. It was a nice sunny day, so I took off my shirt and worked on my tan. This afternoon we (the whole battery) had our pictures taken, and then I got on a detail to clean the guns we used this morning. That was OK by me because it meant a chance to better learn the workings of a gun. After chow we went to the show, "Star Spangled Rhythm." It was so good. Every star on the Paramount lot was in it. I love you and I miss you a whole lot.

XXX, Gib

February 14, 1943, Camp Callan, California

Darling Genie, today after inspection Harvey Peterson and I went to La Jolla. Harvey is a former bank examiner from Milwaukee. We met Roberson and his wife (she's visiting from Chicago) in their hotel, where they let us change our clothes. From there we walked down to the beach in our swimming suits. The Pacific Ocean was pretty cold, so our swim was short. But we had lots of fun crawling around on the rocks and sitting in the sun, chewing the fat. We had dinner together tonight before Pete and I lit out for the barracks. We now have a new lieutenant from Camp Davis. He's 3rd platoon commander. He's just out of O.C.S. and looks like such a nice fellow. Lights are going out.

Goodnight, Darling. I miss you so much, Gib

February 15, 1943, Camp Callan, California

Darling, you mention coming someplace to meet me on my way to Camp Davis. I would certainly like that, Honey, but it can't be done. We'll all go together on a troop train and absolutely no stopovers. I'll get a furlough after O.C.S. but not until then. I will get ten days plus traveling time from Davis to home and then to a new station. That I know for sure. Maybe we can meet in Chicago for a day or two before coming home to Whitewater. Wouldn't it be grand to have each other all to ourselves for a while?

All my love, Gib

February 16, 1943, Camp Callan, California

Darling Baby, official sources indicate we'll have one more week of O.C.S. prep school, a week's hike and maneuvers, and away we'll go to Camp Davis in North Carolina. Before we go, we'll get thirty hours of math and thirty hours of gunnery. Whatever gunnery is. I wish I could have some more preparation. Looking back now, I feel as if the time has gone quickly. Must get at my lessons now.

Good night, Darling, Gib

February 18, 1943, Camp Callan, California

Dearest Baby, after mail call last night, they sprang an alert on us. This means the whole battery has to turn out and go down and set up the guns, ready to shoot down anything in sight. The thing is, we don't know whether it's practice, or if we're playing for keeps. We stayed out until 9:00 when I came back and had an hour's rest before walking my guard post until midnight. Boy, was I tired. Today started with a double-time march to class 15 minutes from here, where we study algebra, logs and trig. Got to study some now. I miss you something awful.

Good night, Darling. Love and XXX, Gib

February 19, 1943, Camp Callan, California

Dearest Genie . . . we had a formal parade today, and every mother's son was in it. The column was sixteen abreast and about six blocks long. Very impressive ceremony. As we marched past the reviewing stand, the band played "Over There," and we were all thinking the same thing: *We won't be back 'till it's over over there"* . . . In other news, we haven't been allowed to bathe all week because they're repairing the water mains. This is a problem because we have to run for about a mile each morning before class and get back to barracks and change into officers' dress uniforms in about five minutes and then get to class about ten blocks away. Glad to hear that the ban will be lifted tonight because it smells like a beaver hut around here.

All my love, Gib

(Gib, having been the drum major of his high-school band, was probably quite skilled when it came to parades and reviews. I imagine the combination of marching music, spiffy uniforms and precise steps gladdened his heart. I think I inherited this trait because my favorite part of kindergarten was marching around the room with my classmates while our teacher played the piano. My report card shows an E for Excellent in the marching column.)

February 21, 1943, Camp Callan, California

Hi there. Gee, do I ever love you. You bet. Another letter from you today. This time with four lipstick kisses on it. I'm on gun crew tonight, and tomorrow I'm barracks guard. That means I have to stay around all day and hold down the fort, keep the waste bucket empty and prevent mayhem. Maybe I'll also have time to straighten out my footlocker, wash out some clothes and study some trig. Tonight, I got into a game of hearts and won a nickel. I love you more and more every day and always will.

XXX, Gib

February 25, 1943, Camp Callan, California

My Darling, as you know, we march to classes in formation each day. Today I was daydreaming and not paying very much attention to the formation. In fact, I was watching a car go by. The lieut. who was marching with us snuck up behind me and bawled the hell out of me for watching traffic when I should have been watching where we were going. He was right to do this. The harder they ride us here, the easier time we will have at O.C.S. We had a test in gunnery. I studied pretty hard, and if I didn't make any foolish mistakes, I should be OK. Did I tell you about my valentine from the gang at the bank? It came in a big thick envelope and included my old mouse trap. If you want to know more about my mouse trap, ask Jim or Alvin or Margie. I must sign off and study electricity now. I don't know very much about electricity so far. I love you and I miss you an awful lot.

I misses your kisses, Gib

(Uncle Jimmy and Alvin Halverson were co-workers at the bank. Jimmy told me the story about the mouse trap. Apparently, one morning Gib discovered a little dead mouse in the trap he'd set on the floor near his cashier's window. Feeling mischievous, he quickly hit upon the idea of putting the mouse in Alvin's cash drawer. He and Alvin, co-founders of the fictitious conglomerate Shady Deals, Inc., enjoyed playing tricks on each other. Alvin had many opportunities to open his cash drawer that morning and, suspecting Gib of having nestled it there, thought it would be fun to ignore the dead mouse peeping out from under the twenty-dollar bills. When Alvin went for an early lunch, Margie Hessleman left her desk in the bookkeeping department to fill in for him. Margie's scream upon opening the cash drawer echoed through the lobby, alarming customers and workers alike. Bernice Joliffe, thinking someone had tried to rob Margie, pressed the burglar alarm in her teller's cage. By the time the police arrived, Gib had stepped in to soothe Margie and cash the customer's check. He apologized to the police about the false alarm and took the rap for the dead mouse incident. He gave an apology to Margie, too, along with a bouquet of roses. Jim said Margie was a famous good sport.)

March 5, 1943, Camp Callan, California

Dearest Genie, Lieut. Carpenter got a wild idea that all the latrines ought to be painted. I figured that was a good detail and volunteered. Took seven men all day to slap paint on those walls. Before, they looked like latrines. Now, they look even worse.

All my love, Gib

March 6, 1943, Camp Callan, California

Dearest Genie, I managed to draw switchboard duty again. I'm on from 6:00 to midnight. All quiet here now. The switchboard is in the Battalion Headquarters Office. The Officer of the Day has to stay here all night and is just now going to bed. Sergeant of the Guards has also made up a cot on the floor. This place looks more like a flophouse than an office right now. I had a fine compliment this evening. Sergeant Brungess, who is in charge of this detail, said he wished he could trust the rest of the men on the switchboard like he trusts me. Then he could sleep all night and know things would be running smoothly. That made me feel good.

All my love, Gib

March 8, 1943, traveling by troop train to Camp Davis, North Carolina

Dearest Genie, I couldn't tell you the details before (due to security). Right now, thirty men from our battery are in this shipment to Swamp Davis. As you can see from the return address, I am now a corporal. That's an automatic promotion for all men going to O.C.S. We got on the train last night at Del Mar, arriving in Los Angeles at midnight. There we got on the car where we'll stay for the rest of the trip. It's a Pullman that's been converted for carrying troops. Rows of bunks in three layers. I'm on the top, just under the roof. I'm sitting in the club car now, writing this. Can you see by my penmanship that the train is waving and weaving like mad? Maybe the engineer is a rookie. I came close to being thrown out of my bunk several times last night on some of the stops he made. There are several perpetual card games going on, so if I get tired of reading and writing letters I can sit in if the stakes aren't too high. Good thing I like ginger ale because that's all they serve on board. War department says so. Seems some civilians get on the trains, get the boys talkative and try to get information out of them. We're just outside of Needles and about to cross over into Colorado. I'm going to try to mail this now in Needles. All my love to you and Baby. I love you so and miss you terribly.

All my love, Pop

March 9, 1943, en route to Camp Davis, North Carolina

My Darling Genie, now we're in Clovis, New Mexico. Soon we cross into Texas and then up through Kansas City and on to St. Louis. Not sure of the route from there. We are the first thirty to be sent on, but we left some mighty nice fellows behind. McCarthy was one of them. Big tall blond Irishman. I guess a person is just as well off not to make many close friends in the army because you can never tell when you'll be separated. How I miss you. After I get those gold bars on my shoulder, you and Baby are coming with me as long as I'm in this country. I'll have an officer's salary then, and we can afford it. All for now, Baby.

All my love to the most beautiful girl in the world. Gib

March 11, 1943, en route to Camp Davis, North Carolina

Dearest Genie, we're laying over in Atlanta. Atlanta is a dump. Last night we wandered around town for a while, found an oyster bar, ate oysters and crackers and drank some beer. This morning, we ate in the station restaurant. Greasy bacon, hominy grits, and underdone scrambled eggs. I've heard that Camp Davis isn't real lovely, but it has to be better than Atlanta. I'd wish you were here, but I wouldn't wish this town on anyone as pretty as you. Maybe I'm just grumpy from riding so long on the train. Good night, my darling.

I love you, Gib

(Gib wrote letters home for two years. The above is the only totally negative letter in his entire body of work. I've lived in Atlanta for the last 53 years and have grown very fond of the place. I wish Gib could come for a visit. We'd get the guest room ready for him. We'd decorate it with photos of Barbara and our young family as we looked in 1942-1944. When he felt like taking a spin around town, I'd show him the High Museum of Art and take him to concerts at Symphony Hall. We'd go to Murphy's or another cozy restaurant in the Virginia Highlands part of town. We'd walk up to the Emory campus, and he could see where my husband had his teaching career and visit the hospital where I did my training to be a hospital chaplain. One weekend, the family would come up from Savannah so Gib could meet his great-grandchildren and their dog. I think Gib might feel differently about Atlanta after this adventure.)

Part Two

Officer Candidate School

March 15 - July 19, 1943

March 15, 1943, Camp Davis, North Carolina

Dearest Genie, what a dump this is. Flat and sandy. We're temporarily in some old tarpaper barracks until tomorrow. I thought Atlanta was bad, but it's Shangri-La compared to this. We left Atlanta on Friday, got to Wilmington Saturday morning and waited for the bus that took us here. I've got the blues something bad tonight. Soon as your letters start coming, I'll feel better.

I love you, Gib

March 17, 1943, Camp Davis, North Carolina

Darling Genie, that's my new address on the envelope. Write me a nice long love letter right now and cheer me up. There's lots of work to do here. I won't be able to write each day like I could in the past. It's going to be tough here, but I think I can make it. That's the theory I'm subscribing to, anyway. Last time I wrote, I was griping about the dirty old place we were in. Well, now we're in the same type of barracks, only it's clean because we've been cleaning it. Keep writing every day, and I'll do what I can. I want to call you and hear your voice, but I don't have the slightest idea where the Western Union office is. I hear that it takes hours to get a call through out of here and I don't have the time to spare.

I love you with all my heart, Gib

March 22, 1943, Camp Davis, North Carolina

My Darling Baby, I've got so much to write I don't know where to begin. But first: I can have you come down here and stay for a while. Next Saturday I'm going to Wilmington to see if I can find a place for you to stay. I can be with you on the weekends. Can you manage to stay over two weekends? Will the grandmas be able to be on duty that long? My morale was pretty low when we arrived, but I'm OK now. Moving into a new outfit where I knew nobody was what got me. Now I know some of the fellows, and they're a pretty good bunch. We are living in T.O. shacks. T.O. stands for theater of operations. A T.O. shack is different than a standard barracks. It's built of one thickness of some asphalt and asbestos siding material. We are studying gunnery, math and several other subjects. Lutheran services take place at this camp, and I see that there is communion tomorrow. Lots to do. Love you lots.

All my love, Gib

(Wilmington, about thirty miles from Camp Davis, had a number of hotels and guest houses to accommodate visiting family members. My mother stayed in one of them for two weeks in mid-April. Gib could leave base and spend all weekend with her, but on weekdays she was on her own. Wisconsin can be chilly and windy in April; I imagine she would have enjoyed the warmer weather in North Carolina.)

March 26, 1943, Camp Davis, North Carolina

Dearest Genie, this morning we studied oblique triangles. That was pretty fierce. We have to know that so we can properly aim anti-aircraft weapons. You asked about graduation. July 8th is the day I get the gold bars if everything goes according to schedule. Yesterday, we had bayonet practice. I hope we don't have to do that again anytime soon. I hope I never have to use a bayonet in battle. I love you and miss you and hope you can come and visit soon.

Always, Gib

March 29, 1943, Camp Davis, North Carolina

Dear Baby, next weekend I'm going to ride the bus to Wilmington (about 30 miles) to arrange for a room for you. I can hardly wait for the two weeks you'll be here. If I don't write this week, it's because we're studying map reading and orientation. I'm going to be studying hard.

All my love to the sweetest girl in the world. Gib

March 30, 1943, Camp Davis, North Carolina

Dear Baby, the lieutenant corrected my posture today while we were marching. He almost had me falling backward before he got through. He got right up behind me and hollered. I thought I had pretty good posture, but I've been wrong about that. I've been having trouble sleeping at night. Can't think why . . . I'm good and tired at lights out, but last night I was still awake at midnight. Maybe I'm getting excited about the possibility of seeing you soon. Now it's time to start polishing things and get to bed.

All my love, Gib

April 1, 1943, Camp Davis, North Carolina

Dearest Genie, as you know, we are studying map reading this week. Lieutenant Fogg is the instructor today, and to make a pun, he doesn't belie his name a bit. He's so foggy on the subject, we can't even see him from the back of the room. Now it's after lunch, and we have a new instructor who will be lecturing for the next four hours on something to do with transits. Tomorrow morning, we go out to do some field work with a transit. Maybe I'll know what a transit is by then. It's been more than four months since I've seen you and Kaaren, and I can only imagine how she's grown. Is her birthmark still bright red? If I had to pick her out of a crowd, probably the only way I could identify her is by that bright red strawberry on her upper left arm. Lots going on here. I might not be able to write until Saturday, when I can let you know about your room in Wilmington.

All my love, Gib

(A transit is an instrument used in surveying. I hope Gib's knowledge of surveying and map making helped him find his way in unknown territory. He was in the Battle of the Hürtgen Forest, where, according to the history of the battle, the army was unaware of a newly built lake in the area. Maps supplied to the troops could be inaccurate, and soldiers would have had to depend on their own skills in cartography.)

April 3, 1943, Camp Davis, North Carolina

Darling Genie, if nothing unforeseen happens, I'll go to town tomorrow to find you a room. I hope I can find an opening. April 10th wouldn't be good because I'll be on the firing range all day, so it won't be that weekend. It will be the next, though, if I can find a place for you. I can be with you on the weekends, but not during the week. You can sightsee, read and rest. Today we had our map reading and orienteering exam. I did fine except for a small mistake in my surveying test. We've seen some training films on chemical warfare and infantry drill this afternoon. Tomorrow, we have a gas demonstration and more training films, then inspection in ranks, then chow and then I hop on a bus to Wilmington to find a guest room for you. It will be swell when you arrive.

All my love, Gib

April 9, 1943, Camp Davis, North Carolina

Darling Genie, I've reserved a room for you in Wilmington. I walked all over town until I found it. All the hotels were completely booked. The room is pretty small and drab but it's only two blocks from the train station at 212 Red Cross Street. It rents for seven dollars a week, so I gave the landlady fourteen dollars. When you arrive, you'll be tired from riding on the train, so take a nap. I may not be there on Saturday until at least 3:00, because we may be on the firing range. Put some perfume behind your ears so I can smell it when I kiss you. The room is nothing like anything at the Palmer House, but it's all I can find until May, and I can't wait that long to see you.

XXX, Gib

(Gib and Geneva had spent the second night of their honeymoon at the Palmer House in Chicago. Still in business today, it retains its vintage vibe and opulent lobby. According to the Palmer House bill in my mom's wedding scrapbook, they paid $7.00 for the overnight and another ten cents for a telephone call on the day of checkout.)

Later on, April 9, 1943, Camp Davis, North Carolina

Darling Genie, did you have a good trip down here? I imagine you're pretty tired after two nights riding in coach. I won't be there until 3:00 at least. Rumors are running wild that we may fire on the range Saturday, and if so, we won't get through until afternoon. I may be as late as 6:00, but I'll get there ASAP. I'm so excited to see you I just tremble thinking of it. It's been so long since I've seen you, I'll probably be all bashful and embarrassed. I doubt it, though. Here's a tip: go downtown and get some groceries because the restaurants are packed on the weekend. If you don't have time, forget it. But if you do have time, pick up some cheese, crackers, fruit, or stuff like that.

All my love, Gib

(Gib sent the above letter to my mom at the guest house in Wilmington. The envelope is addressed to Mrs. H.G. Andersen, 212 Red Cross Street, Wilmington, NC. Google Maps shows a large frame house with upstairs balconies at that address today. It's only three blocks from River Walk, where she might have gone to stroll along the Cape Fear River.)

April 28, 1943, Camp Davis, North Carolina

Dearest Genie, you've only been gone two days, but it seems that many months. It was pretty tough to get on that bus for camp and leave you behind in Wilmington. Hope you got home OK. Tell me about your train ride and all the marines, soldiers and sailors who tried to flirt with you. Darling, I love you so. Kiss Kaaren. Thank Lil for the package.

All my love, Gib

May 3, 1943, Camp Davis, North Carolina

Dearest Genie, I miss you so much more after having you down here for two weeks. Luckily, they keep us busy, and I have little time to think about my loneliness. They are shuffling us around into different batteries and different barracks. We packed all morning, and after chow, trucks came to take us to our various new batteries. I'm in the 31st Battery now, living in a wooden building instead of a tarpaper shack. Myself and a man named Browne, from Brooklyn, have one of the squad rooms in this barracks. I feel awfully depressed tonight. Maybe it's the moving to a new battery, not knowing anyone and missing you. Good night, Darling.

I love you and always will, Your Poppy

May 5, 1943, Camp Davis, North Carolina

Dearest Genie, forget all that morose and gloomy stuff I've been sending. I'm OK now. Got six letters from you today. This is now a wonderful place. I could fight a tiger and give him first bite. I will start studying soon, but I want to let you know that my morale is now OK. It also helps that I got paid yesterday. $72.47 this month. I'll send some home the next chance I get. It's so windy here. The story is told about a farmer living near here whose hen was sitting with her tail to the wind. She laid the same egg six times! Gotta quit now.

Love and XXX, Gib

May 10, 1943, Camp Davis, North Carolina

Dearest, I'm platoon leader this week, and my troubles are numerous. Today we spent the whole day cleaning the barracks. Washed the outside of the building, all the windows, moved two coal bins. I'm about dead. It's hard to motivate men who are already tired from all the work they've done before the cleaning detail. We started moving Friday evening, did all that cleaning, and then went on the firing range, then cleaned all the rifles. I hope I can take all the stuff the officers dish out. I'll be platoon leader until Thursday morning. Keep your wonderful letters coming and tell me more about Kaaren. I'd love to see a picture of her with zwieback smeared all over her face. Good night, Darling.

You know how much I love you. Gib

May 16, 1943, Camp Davis, North Carolina

Dearest Genie, this gunnery course has been the toughest so far. The test this morning seemed easy – too easy. I'm afraid of it for that reason. I finished in one hour, and we had two-and-a-half hours to work on it. Me and two other fellows decided we had to get off base for a day in order to save our sanity. (I hope we're not too late.) The three of us rented a double room in Hotel Cape Fear. I'll let them sleep in the beds and I'll take the floor because, as I might have mentioned, my barracks has a bed bug invasion. It will be better sleeping on a hotel room floor than in the pup tent I'd be staying in while the barracks is being fumigated tonight. The three of us waited for the bus at the Fourth Street Gate, but a captain came along before the bus arrived and gave us a ride into town. I'm here with Browne, my roommate, and J. Gadwell from the 27th battery. Gadwell reserved this room a couple of weeks ago, and Browne and I convinced him that we'd be good company. And he's glad to let us help pay for it. No news to write about. We've been doing the same things day in and day out: riding three miles to class in a cattle truck, studying at night, taking tests, going to the firing range, scrubbing the barracks and getting ready for inspection. Tomorrow, we plan to go to church, have breakfast at The Southern Kitchen and then get back to camp early to get ready for Monday, when we start studying automatic weapons. It sure feels good to be away for even an overnight. I wish you were here, too. We could give Browne and Gadwell some money for ice cream and cuddle up until we hear their feet in the hall.

All my love, Gib

May 20, 1943, Camp Davis, North Carolina

Dearest, I got some bad news. I got a 64 in the gunnery class. Seventy is passing. I don't know what this means for my situation. They may just let it go. Or I may be turned back to start over, or they could relieve me of duty. I don't think they'll do the latter, but I'm feeling ill about it. You'll probably get this on your birthday. I wish I had better news, but I did send you a gift from Wilmington. I remembered you admiring a yellow slip in that ladies' shop near the river, and I found it and sent it to you. I hope it fits. If not, maybe you can take it in? Now it's evening, and I had a chance to talk to my lieutenant about my test score in gunnery. He said it wouldn't affect my position at all unless I flunk another test. How about that for a birthday present? I feel swell now, hearing that from him. Darling, I miss you so much. Graduation is coming. I'll be an officer, and you and baby can come with me to my next posting.

All my love, Gib

May 22, 1943, Camp Davis, North Carolina

My Darling Genie, it's Saturday. Browne and I took off from camp right after chow this noon, and are now at Wrightsville Beach. We got a room for the night at a hotel here. The landlady set up a bed for us in the dining room. Can you imagine that? We picked up two other fellows from our platoon, and the four of us will spend the night in the dining room. There's another bed in there, but we don't know who it's for. We've been swimming and sitting on the beach. We have to be back at the barracks tomorrow by 2:00 to scrub the building on the outside again. I'm writing this at the USO in Wrightsville Beach. It's on an inlet from the ocean and has a huge porch looking out over the water. I love you. You are my everything.

I must close now and write to the other girl I love . . . your daughter and mine. Pop

May 24, 1943, Camp Davis, North Carolina

Dear Kaaren, last time I wrote to you was to thank you for the anniversary card you sent me on the day your mom and I had been married for two years. By now you are nine months old. You have four teeth. You are sitting up, and you are eating solid foods. When I left home, you were still nursing and drinking from a bottle. You were a darling baby then, and I imagine you're even sweeter now. It's been so long since I've seen you. Why am I away learning to be an officer? Well, daughter, we've got quite a job to do before I can come back to you and Mother. I'm doing my part so we can live in peace and security again. When you were born, I promised myself I would do everything I could to keep you and Mother safe, and that's what I'm doing now. There are lots of other fathers in this, too, and I'm sure they all feel the same way. I long for the day I can come home and live with you both again. We'll have lots of fun. We can take Barbara for walks in the woods. We can go swimming in the summer, and we can go sledding on that big hill in the park in wintertime. Maybe we can have a house with a fireplace and screen porch. I'll walk you to school and help you with your homework. Until then, be a good girl and mind your mother. She's a wonderful woman.

I think of you both all the time and can hardly wait to see you! Dad

(We three were all together when Gib got home to White-water on furloughs. And we were able to live together from September through December 18,1943, when Gib was receiving training at Camp Edward, Massachusetts. We also lived together on base at Camp Haan in Riverside, California, and Fort Hood, Texas, from mid-February to early September 1944. From there he shipped out to England and eventually reached the battlefield. I was just two the last time I saw Gib. It would be an exaggeration to say I remember anything about our time together, but sometimes it seems as if a memory is just about to surface, like it does when I wake up in morning unable to remember anything about a dream from the night before, except that it was a happy sort of dream.)

May 25, 1943, Camp Davis, North Carolina

Dearest, no letters from you for four days. I know you're writing them. I'm just not getting them. I hope I get them soon, they mean so much to me. This morning, we were down at the beach working with 40-mm guns. We take them apart and put them back together. Tomorrow we'll get to the 50-caliber machine guns and study them for several days. We can go swimming during the noon hour, and it feels so good to cool off in the ocean. Sometimes the waves are big enough to knock us over. Must get ready for tomorrow.

All my love to you and Baby Kaaren, Gib

May 28, 1943, Camp Davis, North Carolina

Dearest Genie, my morale is way up now. Three of your letters came today. It was wonderful when I walked in and saw those three letters waiting on my bed. You say that Kaaren is always smiling and happy. That's because you're a wonderful mother. This afternoon we had the Automatic Weapons test. It was a breeze. Did I tell you that when we practice firing, our targets are old planes that are being towed by another plane? They don't want us shooting at the real thing, but they want it to seem like the real thing. Now it's the weekend, and I'm at the USO in Wilmington. Browne has gone to see family in Massachusetts. Gadwell is visiting his brother who's stationed at Fort Fisher, and I have you to write to. I got up before anyone else and went swimming all alone. I thought about us and how wonderful it will be when I'm home.

All my love, Gib

June 1, 1943, Camp Davis, North Carolina

My Darling, we're concentrating on the 40-mm gun right now. Today we had parts spread all over the place, and we practiced putting the gun back together. After working with the guns, we ran the obstacle course. I thought I'd die. We'll have to do it again and again, and I hope to improve. Did I tell you about the mosquitoes around here? They come over in formations like dive bombers. They leave us alone on the obstacle course, but as soon as we slow down, they launch another attack. I love you always, sending millions of kisses. Give one to Kaaren.

All my love, Gib

June 5, 1943, Camp Davis, North Carolina

Dearest, I've finally found time to write. Have you wondered what happened to me? The lieut. decided that our barracks were filthy, so we had to scrub every night this week. This week was also the beginning of the automatic weapons (A.W.) course. It's been tough, but the exam tonight was easy. We have three more weeks of A.W. specialization. It's getting to be a grind, and I couldn't take time off to write to you. Sorry, Darling. The end is near. We ordered our new uniforms last night so we can dress as officers when the time comes. Each day we've been learning the tricks of dirty fighting: how to kick, gouge, rip an opponent and use our hands as weapons. This training takes place between 4:00 and 5:00, and we call it "The Hour of Charm."

I hope I never have occasion to put these skills to use. Tomorrow, we don't have inspection but instead will see a mock court-martial trial, so we'll know something about how those things work. They dismissed us early tonight, so I have time to write to you. I love you and miss you more every day.

All my love, Gib

June 6, 1943, Camp Davis, North Carolina

Darling, they took our class picture today. I guess they think we might graduate. I got your Wednesday letter this noon. You were awfully depressed and unhappy then. I know you're having a tough time, my darling, but keep the chin up. I'll try and make this all up to you when the war is over. Right now, everybody has to take a lot of things they don't like. When I get my bars, we can afford to live together in our own space. Next week promises to be pretty tough. We're going to be studying the director, which is an electrical gadget for aiming the gun. It's more elaborate than anything Rube Goldberg ever dreamed of, and we have to be able to take it apart and put it back together.

I love you. Gib

(It would be interesting to read the letter Gib is responding to here. I imagine that Mom missed Gib. I imagine it was exhausting to be the only parent of a toddler. I imagine it might have been challenging to live with her mother-in-law. Even though she had a built-in babysitter, my mom might have longed for her own home, her own kitchen, her own space. Grammy, my other grandmother, spent hours with me, too. I am certain that I benefitted from both of my grandmothers' company, but maybe my mother longed for a more settled routine. I wished I'd asked her what this time was like for her, but I never did. I think I assumed that it had been grand dividing our time between the big white house on Center Street and the big yellow house on Main Street where Barbara had taken up residence, but maybe Mom would have been more comfortable if the two of us had our own small apartment.)

June 12, 1943, Camp Davis, North Carolina

Dearest, I'll try to answer some of the questions in your last letter. Specialization – that means four weeks of concentration on all things related to automatic weapons. This would include gunnery problems, equipment and gun drill. We have finished the 11th week today, and we have two more weeks to go. Then come two weeks of firing. Then on the 16th week we go on maneuvers, and graduation is the 17th week. We scrubbed the barracks again tonight after study hall. When I get home, you will have to let me scrub the whole house twice a week so I'll be able to keep in shape. Have to quit now and get shoes, belt buckle and everything else in shape for inspection tomorrow. Some of the big boys are coming by to inspect us, so we have to do an extra good job. I miss you an awful lot.

All my love, Gib

June 14, 1943, Camp Davis, North Carolina

Dearest, I'm staying in camp this weekend but not by my own choice. Seems the lieutenant found fault with my shoes. He said they weren't well polished, so I am restricted, and it rather cramps my style. In this battery, restricted men have to report to the office every hour, so we can't wander very far away. So, all I've done today is dig ditches and report to the office every hour. My back and shoulders are damn sore, and I can barely move. Did I tell you how much I like that picture of you holding Kaaren? You have on your housecoat, and you look so warm and comfortable. Tell me more about our daughter. Can she stand yet without holding onto things? You are both so precious to me.

All my love, Gib

June 15, 1943, Camp Davis, North Carolina

Dearest, it isn't too early to talk about graduation, is it? We get out of here Thursday, July 22, at noon. Why don't we meet in Chicago on Saturday and spend the weekend in Chicago by ourselves before going on to Whitewater? Would you like that? Or would you rather have me come straight home? I think it would be better if we could be alone for a bit. I'll have enough money saved up by then to swing the deal, so don't worry about that angle. It will be great when I get those gold bars, and the three of us can be together on base (wherever that may be). My work will really begin after graduation, but I'll be able to have you and Kaaren somewhere near me, and that will make all the difference. Maybe I'm a bit premature talking about all of this now, but it's something we can look forward to. Our last written exam will be on Friday, and after that we're being watched by the officers and graded that way. Must sign off now. All my love, Baby. Let me know what you think of my plan.

All my love, Gib

June 17, 1943, Camp Davis, North Carolina

Dearest, how I miss you and the Wisconsin weather. We had a battalion review, and the sweat was rolling down my back like a river. I tried to faint just to get out of it but couldn't. I thought they would be dropping like flies, but I didn't hear anyone keel over. How thrilling to get my first Father's Day gift from Kaaren. The candy and nuts came last night, and the boys have been helping me consume them. Please thank our daughter for me. Now I must polish my shoes, polish my belt, shave, shower and get in bed. I am so tired. I long to be with you.

Kisses, Gib

June 19, 1943, Camp Davis, North Carolina

Darling, what a day. Hope I don't get many more like this. We had a full field inspection this afternoon. That means we take all the stuff we normally take in the field, go out in a sandy field, and put all our equipment out on the ground. Then we pitch our tents next to our displays and stand in the hot sun waiting for the big boys to come and inspect our work. Now it's after chow, and we're in study hall. The instructor is about to read the list of those who flunked the test this afternoon. It was the toughest one we've been exposed to yet. Everyone is sitting on the edge of their chairs and holding their breath. Me too. It's the last test we'll have. From here on in it's all field work, firing on the range, tactical problems. We have another field inspection tomorrow morning. The instructor still hasn't read the results. He seems to be trying to figure something out. He just announced that the only flunk was Browne, my roommate. I'm glad it wasn't me, but at the same time, I'm sorry it was he. He probably will have to be sent back to review and retake the test. I hope not. I'd hate to have to break in a new roommate. I'm looking for the box of goodies you girls are sending to me. I hope it gets here tomorrow so Browne and I can enjoy it over the weekend.

All my love, Gib

June 24, 1943, Camp Davis North Carolina

My Darling, we're spending this week on the range. We're firing everything an Automatic Weapons outfit would have at their disposal and really learning things. The major in charge of our firing is easy to like, and the instructors down there are a nice bunch of fellows who know their business. We're able to relax and learn by doing. They let us go swimming (the range overlooks the ocean) from 11:15 to noon and then we have chow up in the barracks, or we can take sandwiches from the PX down to the beach with us so we can stay near the water longer. I won't be able to write very long letters for a while because we have to stay on the ball now. I love you something fierce.

All my love, Gib

(Although Gib and his fellow soldiers were well trained in automatic weaponry, this skill wasn't very helpful in the Battle of the Hürtgen Forest because the dense cover of trees prevented the weapons from reaching their mark. In earlier letters, Gib wrote about practicing bayonet skills and hand-to-hand combat, hoping that he never had to put those skills to work. Sadly, I think he may have had to.)

June 28, 1943, Camp Davis, North Carolina

My Dearest Genie, it's been days since I last wrote. Since then, I've covered many miles and had many strange adventures. I've been shot at – they've tried to burn me up and blow me up. All last Thursday we were firing at an empty plane that was being towed by another airplane. Thursday night we prepared our packs (including mosquito netting, a complete change of clothing, raincoat, blanket, a shelter-half and toilet articles), filled out buddy sheets, scrubbed the barracks and were in bed at 10:00. Reveille at 5:45. We pulled out of here at 6:30 wearing full packs and worried faces. We hiked about three-and-a-half miles into the swamps behind the airport. The first thing to meet our eyes in this dismal wilderness was an obstacle course the likes of which has never seen life this side of Hell. First, we came upon pine boughs laced together about twenty inches above the ground . . . not quite enough room for a man wearing a backpack to crawl under. But we did it anyway. Next, we met with a barbed wire entanglement stretched over a twenty-foot-wide and five-foot-deep ditch of water. We crossed this by running along on poles placed across the thing. I didn't fall in, but there were those that did. Then we climbed up a twenty-foot-long rope to a platform from which we had to jump down. What did we do then? We pitched tents. Browne and I were together. We finally got the thing up and then had to camouflage it. Then the chow truck came with a horrid concoction. After lunch came the infiltration course. We began by lying in a ditch. At the sound of a whistle, we started crawling forward on our bellies. Why crawl? Because machine guns were firing 30 inches above where we crawled and sticks of dynamite exploded at odd moments. Not wanting to be shot yet, I stayed low and plowed a furrow with my nose. The hot sun beat down on us, baking the sand to a white heat. This was not without its compensations, however. As I crawled along, what should I see in the hot sand but one dollar and sixteen cents. I stopped crawling long enough to pocket this fortune. After all this folderol, we listened to lectures on grenade throwing and making home-grown grenades out of dynamite and gasoline. We had supper out in the woods and slept under the wide canopy of the sky. Whippoorwills, bobwhites and owls called out all night. The mosquitoes didn't bother us because Browne and I had taken the precaution of anchoring our mosquito netting with logs before we retired for the night. We were up before dawn, struck our tents, rolled our packs and were back in the barracks at 7:00. Then we had to get ready for inspection at 11:00. Then came chow, and then I lit off for Wilmington so I could pick up the rain boots you left at the guest house when you were here. I went right to the Post Office with them, but the windows were all closed, so I had to lug them back to base camp with me. I got back with rides from a captain, a lieutenant and a civilian. Now it's Sunday, and I went to the Lutheran church up on 13th and D Streets, and now I've just washed out my filthy fatigue clothes and will soon go to bed. Three more weeks of this, Darling, and I'll be on my way home to you.

All my love to the Sweetest Girl in the world. Gib

(This is an excerpt from one of the longest of Gib's letters. It's full of a young man's enthusiasm for learning new skills and successfully facing challenges. It's also full of unintended irony, because while this training took place in a hot and sandy location, Gib's ultimate challenge would take place in a cold forest with mud deep enough for tanks and trucks to become mired.)

July 1, 1943, Camp Davis, North Carolina

Dearest Genie, it was a real morale booster to order our new officers' uniforms last night. I got pink pants, green jackets, khaki and poplin shirts, shoes, caps, ties, brass bars, gold bars and crossed cannon. I have to go back on Saturday and get my blouse, OD shirts and khaki pants. I only hope I can live up to all that the uniform stands for. Twenty-one days to go until our reunion.

Trembling with excitement, Gib

(During WWII, officers' dress pants, previously true khaki colored, seemed to have a pink cast to them. They wore the pinks with Army green jackets. Their caps could be folded flat. Blouses were meant to be tucked in and "bloused up" a bit. Shirts were a bit more form-fitting. ODs are officers' dress shirts. Gib's fondness for clothing shows up well in this letter.)

July 8, 1943, Camp Davis, North Carolina

Dearest, I got paid today, and I've already spent $15 on my bus ticket to Chicago. We're scheduled to arrive on midnight Friday, but I think we'll be doing well to get there by 3 a.m. Saturday morning. So, get yourself down there Friday night, Darling, and I'll roll in in the wee hours of Saturday morning. I can hardly wait for that moment. If you prefer the Edgewater Beach, let's go there. I'll write and get us reservations so all you'll have to do is arrive and tell them who you are. We'll leave for Whitewater Monday morning. Bring your swimming suit. Maybe we can go swimming Sunday. I'd like to swim in fresh water again for a change. Did I tell you we're out on maneuvers next week, so you won't be getting letters from me during that time? Just found out that I'm power plant operator during maneuvers. That shouldn't be a big deal. Must close now and shine my shoes. See you in two weeks and two days. I love you. You are so wonderful you should have been twins. You have too much beauty and charm for one person.

All my love, Gib

July 10, 1943, Camp Davis, North Carolina

My Darling Genie, the field problem is going to be a tough proposition. We leave Monday morning for Greensboro (about 90 miles away) and set up to defend the airport there. We stay until Wednesday, doing nothing but improving our positions. This means sand bagging, building retaining walls, and getting about six or seven hours of sleep the whole four days. Wednesday evening, we pull out of there, come back to this area and move into a new position at night. On Thursday morning we come back to camp. I must quit now and polish my shoes and belt buckle. I love you madly.

XXXXXXXXXXXXXXXXXXXXXXXXXXXXXX, Poppy

July 12, 1943, Camp Davis, North Carolina

Dearest Genie, we had our pictures taken this afternoon for our officer's identification cards. That was a pretty great morale booster. My serial number will be 0-1057666 when I get the gold bars. I just tried on one of my OD shirts and the sleeves are too long. I could weep. Guess I can have them tailored when I get home. Home . . . what a beautiful word that is! I can't wait for this to be all over, and I can come home to you for good. You and Kaaren. We'll have a wonderful time raising that daughter of ours and getting her married to a man good enough for her. You mention going to the Chicago bus station to meet me. Please don't, Darling. We're getting in at an awfully late hour, and I wouldn't like to have you hanging around a bus station at that time of night. No, Darling, I'd like it a whole lot better if you would go right to the hotel and wait for me. Put on a pretty nightie, dab some perfume behind your ears, curl up in bed with a good book and wait for me. See you two weeks from this morning. Wheeee!

All my love, Gib

July 18, 1943, Camp Davis, North Carolina

Dearest, the big news today is that our stations were announced. Camp Edwards, Massachusetts, is where we're going, Baby. It's not far from Cape Cod. Rumor has it that all men going to Edwards will go in gun batteries. All this time I've been studying automatic weapons, but I don't know much about guns. I'll have to start all over learning the 90 mm and how it works. This morning, we signed our discharges, our commissions and our identification cards. I wanted to get myself a tropical worsted uniform but couldn't find one here. I think I can get that in Chicago. Speaking of Chicago, I made our hotel reservations. I'll see you there, Darling. I can hardly wait.

All my love, Gib

(Just a day after writing this last letter from Camp Davis, Gib and his fellow O.C.S. candidates became lieutenants in the U.S. Army. After graduation, they immediately began ten days of furlough before reporting to their next postings. I'm guessing that my parents had a happy and romantic reunion in Chicago and that my relatives had the red carpet rolled out when they arrived at the Whitewater train station two days later. Probably Barbara found a way to join the welcoming party. Maybe I did, too.)

Part Three

Camp Edwards, Massachusetts

August 4 - December 20, 1943

(Gib spent late July of 1943 at home on furlough. He left no record of that time, but I can imagine he enjoyed being there as much as his family and friends enjoyed having his company. Photos indicate that he took Barbara for canoe rides around the lake and that he, Mom and I played together on blankets in the garden and took walks around town with me in my stroller. I am sure that both of my grandmothers would have hosted family supper parties. When furlough was over, Gib reported to his new posting at Camp Edwards, Massachusetts. The camp originally was a training ground for the National Guard but was acquired by the U.S. Army in 1940, when it was expanded and reconfigured into a training facility for soldiers on the way to battles in Europe. Between 1943 and 1945 [the time of Gib's posting], 40,000 men were processed through this center.)

August 5, 1943, Camp Edwards, Massachusetts

My Darling, here I am at Camp Edwards. The train was delayed due to a wreck between Albany and Boston – we didn't have the wreck. Some other train ahead of us did. We got to Boston three hours late to find it hotter than Camp Davis ever thought of being. But out here on Cape Cod it's nice and cool. The trip out here was uneventful except for my encounter with the girl going from Chicago to Portland. She sat across from me and told me her troubles with her boyfriend in the corps and her stepfather who is no good. I felt sorry for her. I think she needed the ears of a stranger. She exited, and a Canadian took her place. He is an oculist and veteran of the last war. Knowing I was in banking, he was interested in discussing rates of exchange between Canadian and U.S. currency, and he insisted on taking me to the dining car for breakfast and paying my check. Camp Edwards appears to stretch for miles on end. Right now, I'm in something called a Casual Officer's Pool. It's a temporary arrangement until all the other new O.C.S. grads make their way to camp. This morning, I signed a voucher for my travel pay and walked around 53 miles around the post. Found the billeting officer and got a line on a place for us three to stay in Falmouth. It will be swell when we can live together for a while. Right now, we are quartered in a regular barracks just like the ones at Callan and Davis. There isn't much to do yet. It would be a good time to relax except that I can't because I'm too nervous and excited about the newness of this place. Please write me at the address on this envelope.

Love from your adoring husband, Gib

August 6, 1943, Camp Edwards, Massachusetts

My Darling, not much to do as we wait for other officers to report. This gives me lots of time to notice how much I miss you and Baby. I miss Kaaren now more than before. When I left last winter, she was more like a toy than a person. Now that she is a little older, she has become a real being. I was so surprised when I walked into her room that Sunday night when we got home. Such a big girl she is. You are certainly a wonderful mother to raise such a fine girl as that. More officers are arriving in the Casual Officer's Pool, and I'm glad to see that we now have enough for three tables of bridge. Soon I will go into Boston to see if I can buy a car for us to use when you come next month. I swoon to think of it. Your arrival, not the car.

All my love, Gib

August 8, 1943, Camp Edwards, Massachusetts

My Darling, I did it: I bought us a 1940 Plymouth Coach with a blue finish. Price: $675. I got to Boston on the troop train running from Camp to Boston to New York. I stopped at the filling station across the street from the Boston station, and the man there told me to ride the streetcar to a place on the outskirts of town where I purchased the car. That car will carry me from camp to spend weekends with my family. Before that it will get me around to look at places for us to rent. It won't be long now, Darling, until you're here with me.

All the love in the world from your adoring husband, Gib

August 10, 1943, Camp Edwards, Massachusetts

I don't think I mentioned that here at Camp Edwards, the marching band wakes us up at 5:45 every morning by marching all over the place and tooting their brains out. This afternoon, I was in charge of a hiking detail. We went about five miles out and five miles back. Nothing was accomplished on the hike except it gave us some exercise as we continue to wait for all new officers. Now I'm the duty officer, so I'm stuck here until retreat at 5:00 tomorrow afternoon. I have to see that no one burns down the building, and I have to welcome all new officers who may arrive tomorrow morning. Four of us, Wilkie, Rothschild, Barker and me, are having a continuous bridge tournament. Wilkie is my partner, and so far, we're taking a beating. I'm starting to get used to this life of luxury. Getting to work again is going to be pretty hard to take. Now that we finally have hot water, I'm going to treat myself to a nice long shower. I can hardly wait till you get here, and I hope it will be soon.

All my love, Gib

August 12, 1943, Camp Edwards, Massachusetts

My Darling, we are the only outfit in the whole army that can boast having a full colonel for a mail orderly. We are attached to the 64th Anti-Aircraft Brigade, and they have no troops yet, so all the colonel has to do is look after us lieutenants. He delivers the mail to our barracks twice a day. We filled out pay vouchers today. I'm having it all sent directly to the bank. I'll be paid a little more than $300, so we'll be pretty well off financially and can afford to rent something near camp. The car is registered in both our names. I tell you all these things so you will know what's going on. Our bridge game is busted up because Wilkie was pulled out of the pool and assigned a job supervising Radio Controlled Aerial Targets (RCATs). Lamb stew is on the menu tonight, and some of us boys have decided we've had enough of that. "Prune Face" Buckley has a car and will drive us to the Daniel Webster Inn in East Sandwich. I hope they have lobster. I've taken care of the car insurance so I can pick it up Saturday and start looking for our next home. Won't that be swell?

All my love, Gib

(The Daniel Webster Inn is still there in East Sandwich, as it has been for three hundred years, and its restaurant is highly rated today. I hope Gib, Prune Face Buckley and the boys found lobster on the menu in 1943.)

August 14, 1943, Camp Edwards, Massachusetts

My Darling, first I'll tell you about Richard P. Arnold, and then I'll tell you about the house. Arnold is a fellow I know at camp. (We call him "Little Ears," because, as you might guess, he has little ears.) He's a good guy, and he's also looking for a house near camp for his wife and baby daughter. We decided to go in together to save some money and also to provide a place where you and Kaaren will have some company when we dads are away at camp, Monday through Friday. We call it The Mansion, and it's in Buzzard's Bay, about ten miles from camp. You'll just love this place. Four bathrooms, too many bedrooms to count, big kitchen. Two-car garage, private beach. The beach won't be so much in the winter, but it's worth talking about – it's worth about $300 a month, but the woman who owns it only wants $100. Arnold and I had seen the ad for this place but hadn't looked at it because it sounds more like a small hotel than a home. We drove all over the cape yesterday, found nothing and got back to camp dead tired and awfully discouraged. This morning, we set out again. Arnold suggested we look at this place just in case, and you could have knocked us over with a feather. The property goes right down to the bay. Our landlady (Mrs. Smith) says a ten-minute walk will get you to a shopping center, but you'll always have a car because "Little Ears" and I both will have cars. We'll leave one at home and ride to camp together in the other. It's a dandy setup. We were disappointed that the house won't be available until Oct. 1. That's too long to wait for your arrival, so I'm going to find a place for us to stay in the meantime. I could not stand waiting for my two girls that long.

All my love, Gib

August 16, 1943, Camp Edwards, Massachusetts

Dearest Genie, well, I'm duty officer again, and I've been a busy boy all afternoon. People and mail coming and going: people delivering telegrams, officers signing in and signing out and me signing papers right and left. This feels like a good experience, so I rather enjoy it. We start school Monday. Real school, that is. What we've been doing so far is just sitting around waiting for the others to show up and reading various field manuals. That's why I've been able to get off all this time to go house hunting.

All my love to my beautiful wife. Gib

August 16, 1943, Camp Edwards, Massachusetts

Dearest, we now have 68 second lieutenants in the pool. Rumor has it we will be in the pool for about six months before being attached to an outfit. That's good. We'll get all the school out of the way, and when we do get attached, we can concentrate on taking care of the battery.

Can hardly wait for your arrival. I wonder how Kaaren will like riding on a train. It might involve more sitting than she is used to.

Can't wait for you to get here. Your Poppy

August 17, 1943, Camp Edwards, Massachusetts

My darling, Buckley and I went into Falmouth to take some stuff to the cleaners. We returned after 5:00 (retreat time) and were stopped by an MP. We were wearing field jackets, and it seems that field jackets are not to be worn outside of camp after retreat. I was actually sorry for the M.P. He was so embarrassed about stopping officers and correcting them. I thanked him for stopping us because I didn't know about that deal at all. Us rookie officers sometimes don't realize that we're out of uniform. School is in a much more convenient place here at Edwards. We only have to march about twenty yards to class. Can't wait for the weekend so I can find temporary housing as we wait for the mansion to become available.

All my love, Gib

August 18, 1943, Camp Edwards, Massachusetts

Dearest, Arnold and I went out to the mansion again tonight to visit with Mrs. Smith. She will leave everything but towels for us, so you don't have to bring sheets, tablecloths or things like that. No baby beds or playpens are in the house, so I guess you'll have to send them. One more thing to bring: all the clothes hangers you can get your hands on. Mrs. Smith told us she was taking all of hers with her, so be sure to bring some. Please bring our iron and radio, too. I didn't see an iron in the laundry area. I did see a radio, but it is out of order. Did we ever have a tough exam this morning! You should have heard the groans as we got the tests. I'm tired tonight. I think I'm getting soft from all the recent inactivity. Good night now.

Your Loving Husband, Gib

(My mother had to ride three days on a train with an eleven-month-old and luggage containing all our clothing, an iron, a radio, towels and clothes hangers. It could have been a challenging trip.)

August 21, 1943, Camp Edwards, Massachusetts

My Darling Baby, I finally got the license plate, and my gas rationing application papers. I won't be able to get the gas coupons until Monday, but I have enough gas from the coupons I got at home to carry me over the weekend. I can go out tomorrow afternoon and find a little apartment for my babies to live in until we move into the mansion. When you do come down here, plan to get a train that will get you into Boston on a Saturday evening so that I will be sure to be there to pick you up. More tomorrow.

All my love, Gib

August 23, 1943, Camp Edwards, Massachusetts

Dearest, I've got a room for us! Yep, it's true. Mrs. Smith's real estate agent suggested this place. I went out to meet the landlady, and she was very agreeable. I told her about Kaaren, and that seemed to be alright with her. The place was very neat and clean, but the rooms were occupied, so she can't show me anything until Monday. I'll give you the lowdown Monday after chow.

All my love forever, Gib

August 24, 1943, Camp Edwards, Massachusetts

My Darling, it was so wonderful to hear your voice on the telephone tonight. It's so wonderful to know that at last you're coming out here. Along with the other items you're packing, could you also bring my wristwatch and some of my old clothes, so I have something to bum around in during weekends at the mansion? Just a pair of pants and a couple of sweaters – the sort of thing I used to wear when putting on the screens in the spring and storm windows in the fall. This place in which I have a room for you is a real old house, but it's very nice and clean. Our room is on the end of the house, right next to the bathroom. Arnold's wife and baby may stay here, too, but she won't be able to come until the middle of September because she's having an operation of some kind. The house is in a pretty deserted area, but there's a place just down the street where you can get breakfast. I'll be able to get over every night to take you out for a decent meal. I'll see you very soon! Good night now.

All my love, Gib

(I try to imagine our reunion at the train station in Boston. Maybe I was tired and cranky. Maybe Mom was disheveled and exhausted. I think my dad was relieved we'd finally arrived and delighted to have us all together again. I wonder what it was like to live in a remote boarding house for two weeks before the beach house became available. I wonder what it was like to share the mansion with the Arnolds from October 1 until late December, and I wonder what became of them after our adventure together on Cape Cod.)

Part Four

Camp Davis, North Carolina

January 6 - February 14, 1944

(Sometime during his Christmas furlough at home in Whitewater, Gib learned that his next posting would be back at Camp Davis, where he would take part in an automotive course. I can easily imagine it being difficult to leave home and family again and return on his own to what may have been his least favorite camp. He would be there only about six weeks, not long enough to secure a rental home for all three of us.)

January 6, 1944, Camp Davis, North Carolina

My Darling, it's only been three days since I kissed you goodbye in the driveway on Center Street, but it seems that many years. It's been so long since I've done this writing stuff that I'm rather out of practice. Camp Davis hasn't changed much . . . it's still flat and sandy. It's not such a bad place, and I will only be here until the middle of February, so I'll just get on with it. Vaughn Monroe is playing at a Seabee camp in Rhode Island tonight. I have our radio right here, and I'm listening to it. Maybe you are, too. Tomorrow, we drive trucks. The object will be to see how much mud and sand we can go through without getting stuck. Now I will take a hot shower. It will help my cold. I miss you so much. Baby, too.

All my love, Gib

January 7, 1944, Camp Davis, North Carolina

Hello, Darling. This morning, we went north from camp and believe it or not, there are actually some hills up that way. Not steep ones, but hills anyway. We all drove 2-and-a-half-ton trucks. They handle like cement mixers. Tomorrow, we play in the mud holes. I am getting some good use out of my boots.

All my love to you and Kaaren, Gib

January 10, 1944, Camp Davis, North Carolina

My Darling, this afternoon we had more fun than ever so far. We took the trucks through the woods. No roads, no nothing! We just put the things in front-wheel drive and took off. Once I had to drive between two trees with only about an inch of space on each side. Those trucks will go anywhere. I am sorry to hear about Kaaren's cough. I know you'll have her all better in no time. She's such a cute little girl. I miss her so much. More than ever before because she's grown from a little baby to a personality now. I miss you both so much.

All my love, Gib

January 11, 1944, Camp Davis, North Carolina

My Darling, we went driving the big trucks today. I was riding with a character named Santangini and I urged him to drive through a particularly big mud hole. Did we ever get stuck! The truck just dug itself in and there we sat. Another truck came and pulled us out. 1 drove, too, but couldn't get us stuck again. For supper tonight we had fried ham, fried potatoes, fried cabbage, fried cucumbers. (I think that's what they were.) Strictly stinko. Food isn't great here, but there are some fine fellows. Four of us have a breakfast club. Keller is the getter upper: he passes my bunk on the way to the latrine, and on his way downstairs he also gets Sesko and Spence up. Sesko is from the south side of Chicago, and Spence and Keller are from Pittsburgh. Spence is about my age and is going to be a father soon. Keller is over 30, also married but no children. Sesko is single. We four are usually the first ones in the mess hall, so we get our eggs and coffee while they're still hot. I must close now and study a little bit for tomorrow's exam. Missing you and Baby.

All my love to the most wonderful girl in the world. Gib

(It's good that Gib had some experience in the mud. Most of France, Belgium and Germany were mired in mud when he was there during the fall and winter of 1944. My husband and I toured the site of the Battle of the Hürtgen Forest in 2018 and were startled to see tire and tank tracks still visible deep in the soil and old abandoned fox holes on the forest floor. Although we were there 74 years after Gib and his battalion's time, we could easily imagine hearing their shouts and smelling the smoke of their guns.)

January 13, 1944, Camp Davis, North Carolina

I'm a wreck. Battered, bloody and bruised. Tonight, we went out on a blackout convoy over the roughest 15 miles of road in the whole state of North Carolina. I had to wear my helmet because my head was bouncing on the roof of the truck. Listen, Kid, send me that income tax blank, will you? I know for sure that we don't have to pay tax, but I think I have to file a return anyway. I'm tired tonight. I wish you were here. You're such a nice cozy little cuddle bug. I wish Kaaren were here, too. I miss her cute antics and accompanying sound effects. My favorite is her "Bata batta" noise.

I love you and love you and love you, Gib

January 14, 1944, Camp Davis, North Carolina

My Darling, I don't know how to say it, but I guess the best way is to just start. I was terribly disappointed in something you said in the letter I got today . . . the short one written on the insurance note paper. You were wondering why you hadn't gotten any letters from me for two days and thought it was because I hadn't written. And you said that if that was the case, then you would not write either. My Dear, anytime I don't write there will be a good reason for it, so please, please don't ever say anything like that again. There, that's over. Now just forget it. I get just as disappointed when I go several days without hearing from you, but I know that something got snarled up, and it's not because you haven't written. Please, Darling, believe me – I love you more than anything. I miss you so much tonight I could cry. I am glad to hear that Kaaren's cough is better now. That must be a load off your mind. I must go to bed now. Remember that I love you. You are the most wonderful girl in the world. And I ain't just saying that either. It's the truth.

Poppy

January 15, 1944, Camp Davis, North Carolina

Dearest, the fine fellows of the Breakfast Club know how to deal with a rainy Sunday. We went bowling, and I was my usual sloppy self and took a great kidding. Since it was raining, I wore my boots which have rubber half-soles. Bowling in them was not so good. After our time at the bowling alley, we had some supper and then watched the most awful double feature I've ever seen. I wish I could remember the titles because then I could tell you so you could avoid them. If I hadn't been sitting in the middle of the row I would have walked out. I have an awful time getting to sleep around here. I usually watch the clock until past 12:30. Don't know what the matter could be. I think it has to do with missing you so much.

I love you with all my heart, Your Husband

January 18, 1944, Camp Davis, North Carolina

Dearest Genie, tomorrow we get half-tracks and the next day, full tracks. A full track is nothing more than a big tractor that seats about 10 men (a gun crew) and is covered with armor plating and pulls a big gun. They can go anyplace and pull anything and, incidentally, they have Waukesha engines in them. I've seen a lot of equipment that came from around home: Allis Chalmers, A.O. Smith and such. Makes me proud of our little corner of God's green earth. We've been working outside all day making weekly inspections on trucks. That means partially taking the trucks apart and then putting them back together again. Next week we do semiannual checks on trucks, when we take everything apart and then reassemble it again. I've never been much of a vehicle kind of guy, but it is fun to learn something new. When I get home, I'll be able to tinker with our car. I'll be able to take it apart and put it back together again. The Breakfast Club gets up early, so I'd better get to bed. I go happily because I got three letters from you today.

All my love, Gib

January 22, 1944, Camp Davis, North Carolina

My Darling, today we had a trick pulled on us that is typical of this post. Seems that Lt. General McNair is coming down this weekend to inspect the post, so we all have classes tomorrow (Saturday!) until 3:00. To impress the general, our squad will do tomorrow afternoon just what we were doing this afternoon – pulling the tread off a half-track vehicle. Our instructions are to pull the thing halfway off and sit tight until the sentry reports that the big boy is on the way. Then we all grab tools and crawl under the truck and look busy. Can you blame us for being bitter? This morning was more interesting. We were trouble shooting. We had a couple of trucks that wouldn't work, and we had to find out what was wrong and repair them. They were really battered up! Had about five things wrong with them, but we figured it out. Next, they're going to make welders out of us so we can repair vehicles in the field. Darling, you're the loveliest, most wonderful woman in the whole world. You are cute all over, if you don't mind me saying so. You are the light of my life. I love you. I miss you.

As always, your loving husband, Gib

January 24, 1944, Camp Davis, North Carolina

Dear Wife, as you know by now, I've been trying to call you all day. I didn't have anything particular to say, but I wanted to hear your voice. This morning, after breakfast, I went over to the day room which has an outside telephone and started the process. The operator told me I'd have a six-hour delay at least. Well, me being a confirmed optimist, I hung around there all day waiting for the operator to call me. So, you know what happened then. You weren't home when I finally got the call through. I was so disappointed. Better luck next time. I sent you a telegram so that you would know I didn't have anything vital to discuss. School is over in three weeks! Then home to my baby and our baby. I can hardly wait to see you again. After my leave we'll go to my next post, and I'll get back to work helping to win this war.

All the love in the world to my darling wife. Gib

January 25, 1944, Camp Davis, North Carolina

My Darling, what a boring day. Positively horrid. This morning's topic was "Hand Tools." The captain who was instructing discussed the machinist's hammer in great detail. Then it got really boring when we had a lecture on how to use a spray gun followed by a film of a guy spray-painting a truck. This was followed by a trip to the paint shop where we got to practice sanding a truck to prepare it for paint. Then we got to practice using a spray gun. All of the above took most of the day. Since we may finish Automotive School in about two weeks, I've spent the evening doing something very interesting: planning my route home. I'll go through Pittsburgh, spending Friday night with a fellow who lives there. Then I probably should be able to make it home on Saturday. Baby, I can hardly wait to be home in your arms again.

I love you, Darling, with all my heart, Poppy

(Until I read this letter, I'd assumed Gib had traveled to North Carolina by train. Now it's clear how the Breakfast Club members managed their adventures off post. Gib had brought the used Plymouth he'd bought when we were at Camp Edwards with him to Camp Davis.)

January 26, 1944, Camp Davis, North Carolina

Dearest Genie, well, now I'm a machinist and a welder. We spent all afternoon in the machine shop making some gadget to use in the shop. I got all the parts made, drilled the holes, cut threads on two bolts and on the parts. Then came the big moment. I was ready to assemble it. You can imagine with what trembling hands and bated breath I approached this last step.

Can you also imagine the bitter heartbreak and despair when the thing refused to fit together properly? Tonight, I worked for two hours with the innards of a big truck and a hot welding torch. Hard work but successful outcome . . . I got a letter from Pa today. Thank God I'm not as far away as he is! I'll be home in two more weeks and a few days. I can hardly wait. You're everything to me.

All my love, Gib

(My paternal grandfather, Col. Harold Gilbert Andersen, SR., a veteran of WWI, was in charge of a supply depot near Brisbane, Australia, for some time during WWII. I have a Christmas card he sent from there in 1943, and for a long time I had a toy Koala bear he brought home for me in 1945. The cuddly koala was my bedmate when I spent the night at Lanny and Colonel's house.)

February 1, 1944, Camp Davis, North Carolina

My Darling, today we cleaned a mine field. We searched for the mines—and defused them. Don't worry, they weren't live. We also learned how to load trucks onto trains. Tomorrow is the day we find out where we're going from here. I hope it's not here or Stewart. Guys who get sent there go without furlough. If I don't get home, I don't know what I'll do! You are the whole world to me. I will try to make our time together after the war as perfect as possible. You may get tired of having me around, but I will try, with all my heart, to make you happy.

All my love, Gib

February 4, 1944, Camp Davis, North Carolina

Dearest One, I'm still in agony. The assignments haven't come out yet, and I still don't know where I'm going next. I'm hoping and praying it's not Stewart or Davis. This morning, we did spot checks on various vehicles around here. Here's how it works . . . a spot-check crew swoops down on a motor pool and finds everything they can wrong with that pool's trucks. Sort of like bank examiners, only carrying tools instead of pencils. This afternoon, Field Officer Todd spent much of the afternoon lecturing us about field ranges (the kind you cook on). Next week we go out on two all-day convoys. Maybe we can use our field ranges. I got called to the office today and there met a Captain Massey, who was interviewing a bunch of officers for jobs here on this post in the Automotive School. I asked him, just on a chance, if he had the right Andersen. He didn't. He had the file of another Andersen in the same course, and that's who the captain thought he was talking to. Boy, did I shag my tail out of there in a hurry. I'm still shaking.

Guess who I love? Pop

February 5, 1944, Camp Davis, North Carolina

My Darling, I'm coming home. Oh, Baby, I'm so happy. I'm going to try and call you tomorrow. I'm going to Camp Haan. Travel pay for all three of us from East Coast to West Coast. I'm so excited I can't think straight. Keller is going to Haan, too; Spruce is going to Bliss; Sesko is going to Stewart. Poor Sesko, we all say. I'm too excited to write any more. Wheeee! Home!!

(Gib had furlough at home in Whitewater, and in mid-February of 1944, the three of us traveled to Riverside, California, for Gib's posting at Fort Haan. Lieutenant and Mrs. Keller were there too. Camp Haan was in Riverside next to March Army Airfield. It opened in 1941 as an Artillery Anti-aircraft Replacement Training Center and could house 80,000 soldiers. It closed after the war and is now home to a cemetery and a golf course. After several months at Camp Haan, we and the Kellers moved on to Fort Hood in Texas, built in 1942 and still in commission today. With its more than 100,000 acres and wide-open spaces, it remains an ideal place for training troops in skills required for operating tanks and other large pieces of equipment. We were with the Kellers from February to early September that year and seem to have become good friends. I remember getting Christmas cards from them for years after the war was over.)

"I'll always remember how Gib and I became acquainted. It was at Automotive School in Camp Davis, and it was 5:30 in the morning. As I was passing his bed, he bounded up, rubbed his eyes, and growled, 'Hey, wait a minute and I'll go down to chow with you.' I sat down on the edge of his bed and waited while he dressed. We never missed a meal together after that for the rest of the course. I have met thousands of men in the Army, but count few as my friends – Gib was one of the few. He really was a swell guy. I didn't have the pleasure of knowing Gib long, but I learned to love him in the short time we had together. I thought an awful lot of him and felt very badly when I heard the news."

Part Five

Moving toward the Front

September 16 - November 23, 1944

(After our time together at Camp Haan and Fort Hood, my mom and I went home to Whitewater. Gib was in touch, but due to security issues, unable to impart much information about his whereabouts. It is clear he was someplace on the East Coast and probably about to ship out to Europe. One of the following letters implies that my mother stayed with a friend named Helen Jane in Washington D.C. in hopes of spending some time with Gib before he finally departed for Europe. The first U.S. troops had entered Nazi Germany on September 11, 1944. Gib and his battalion arrived in England in late September and from there gradually traveled through France and Belgium and crossed the border into Germany on November 17, 1944.)

**September 16, 1944, censored location,
return address is in care of Postmaster, NY, NY.**

Dearest, the address on the envelope is where you can send mail. You can't come up here for censored reasons. Nor can I tell you where I am. We've been busy all-day, processing and being processed. I got a shot in the arm this afternoon that was about the right size for a horse. This evening, all five of us company officers spent the whole evening censoring the enlisted men's letters. This morning, we listened to orientation lectures. Tomorrow we don't do much except get up for reveille. That's our colonel's idea. He doesn't care if we like him or not. All he does is take movements across the Atlantic and back.

You know how much I love you, Darling, Gib

Later September 16, 1944, censored location

Dearest, I'm squeezing in a few lines whenever I can. As I said in the earlier letter, this place is strictly utter secret. You'd better head for home when you get tired of staying with Helen Jane. Here's a dirty trick. When I got down to the depot after leaving you that last night we were together, I found my train didn't leave until after 11:00. I could have been with you that much longer. From then on, my movements have been secret. I can't even call or send you a telegram. That can't be done yet around here. Your letters should start coming in on Monday or Tuesday. No more sketches. They might be code.

But I can tell you for sure that I love you, Gib

September 21, 1944, censored location

My Darling, here I sit with all sorts of hot information but nothing I can write about. Censoring the mail of the men in the company makes me realize what the difficulties are in writing. Some of those guys have quite a struggle. Don't like that censor's job. Don't like snooping in others' affairs. I go through most of it so fast that I don't get the full sense of the letters, and that's good. I've been going through my stuff, and I find a lot I've got to get rid of. One thing is the service prayer book and psalms that Pastor Suby gave me. They both contain my name, hometown, induction date and oodles of other information the enemy would like to know if I were captured. So, I'll have to cut those pages out of the books. We are processing the men and have issued new clothes to all of them. Now all we have to do is wait for the boat to whistle. I can't tell you much, but I can say:

All my love to the most wonderful girl in the world. Pop

September 24, 1944, somewhere in the Atlantic

My Darling, I'm sitting on the boat deck with the sun shining all over me. Sunny, but cold. I'm wearing my field jacket buttoned up to the neck. I have the new-type jacket, which you may remember seeing in Fort Hood. Same length as a short coat with a drawstring at the waist. Much warmer than the old type. Didn't get a letter from you before leaving the States. That was something of a disappointment, but it means that I'll have that many more letters waiting to catch up with me somewhere on the other side of this big blue ocean. Yesterday was Kaaren's second birthday. Two years old and the sweetest baby there is. You've been such a wonderful mother to her and sometimes father too. You'll have to be both now for a bit longer. We carry on enough training now to keep the troops occupied. I am company censor and orientation officer. That means I keep them informed about the world situation and what to expect when we reach our destination. Foreign monetary information, local customs and such. The officers in my company are all a pretty good bunch. We will all go to separate places when we get to our destination. Your allotment of $190 is supposed to begin on October 1. That is, you should get the first check about that time. Darling, it seems ages since I said goodbye to you in Washington. The last thing you said to me was "God bless you." That was a very wonderful thing to say. This letter reaching you means that I've landed safely.

All my love to my darling wife. Gib

(When Gib, his fellow officers and the enlisted men in their care reached England they took their places in replacement pools. Heavy losses required a ready source of new soldiers. The replacement pools were designed to get fresh fighters where they were needed in the European theater. The need was so great that many soldiers found themselves functioning outside their areas of expertise. Gib, for instance, had been trained as an anti-aircraft specialist, but in his last months of army life found himself in the infantry. Gib and his comrades didn't know which battlefield they'd eventually enter, but they knew they'd gradually find their way to the front. The voice of Gib's letters from September through November of 1944 is similar in tone to his earlier letters. He's the same curious, good-humored and somewhat extroverted young Midwesterner writing home to his wife in Wisconsin. But now he's writing from England, France, Belgium and Germany. Aware that he's getting closer and closer to the battlefield, he still seems to relish his adventures, telling stories about bicycling in the English countryside, sipping white wine and strong coffee in French cafes, having his watch repaired in a Belgian jewelry shop and walking four miles to take a shower in Germany. He moves closer and closer to the action and plays bridge in tents with other young lieutenants while bombs fly overhead. He never expresses any anxieties and always maintains that his postwar plan is to come home and resume family life.)

October 6, 1944, somewhere in England

Dearest, couldn't write last night, spent the whole evening censoring the enlisted men's mail. Over here, we have to take care of the men before we can take care of ourselves, and that's as it should be. We now have to wear neckties. Seems like the closer we get to the real thing, the dressier we get. I'll probably go into battle dressed in pinks and blouse. The noise in here is like high noon in a boiler factory. I can't remember what I was going to write. The food here in camp is the best army food I've had yet. Seems the closer we get, the better attention and care we receive. Your airmail letters have started to arrive. It seems to take them about six days of travel. I am so happy to have them. I sure was lucky to meet up with a sweet little girl like you.

All my love to the sweetest girl in the world and the sweetest daughter. Gib

October 9, 1942, somewhere in England

Dearest One, you should have been here last night to keep me warm. We're sleeping in pyramidal tents and there was a heavy frost last night. No stove in the tent. I had about seven blankets under me and five over me, but that wasn't enough. Our outfit traveled by train to where we are, and you should see the railroad equipment. It looks like a toy train I would buy for Kaaren. The RR coaches are divided into compartments like in the movies. We four platoon officers rode in one compartment with all our gear. Abercrombie slept in just about every position except a headstand. Went through Nottingham but didn't see Robin Hood or Little John. Baby, I got two letters from you today. I also got a letter from Pastor Suby today—a prayer book and a list of APOs of church men, neither of which I'll use. I believe in prayers, yes, but can't see reading them out of books. And I don't know any of the servicemen. Could you see if you can find a Bible small enough for me to carry in my pocket, but big enough to read? I think I will sleep warmer tonight. This afternoon we got some straw to put on our cots. We have a big sack called a mattress cover and we can stuff that with the straw.

I close now, loving you more than ever, Gib

October 10, 1944, somewhere in England

My Darling, it's 9:45 in the evening, and I've just finished censoring a whole big box of mail. My, how these men write! Went to a town near here last night with Burchfield. We couldn't find much to do until we wandered into a pub and got into a double cribbage game with a couple of Britishers. We may go to church tomorrow morning at a big cathedral in another town near here . . . too close to mention its name. Looks like we may never have enough time to get into London. I think of you always. I'm so glad I have such a wonderful wife as you to come home to when this is over. You are always in my prayers. Kiss Baby for me.

All my love, Gib

October 11, 1944, somewhere in England

I'm sitting in our "Officers' Club" tonight writing this. And that belongs in quotation marks. You should see the place. It's a Nissen hut, which is nothing more than a half cylinder of sheet iron boarded up at both ends. Inside are four long tables, and every chair is occupied. The place opens every night at 7:00 and every chair is filled at 7:01. Have you sold the car yet? What are the latest devilments our little Kaaren has gotten into? Honey, how I wish I were with you tonight. You are so cute. Yes, you are, too. We've got to have a home with a fireplace.

All my love, Gib

October 14, 1944, "Officer's Club" somewhere in England

Dear Genie, oh, what a happy day! Got three letters from you. I can't answer any of the questions you may have asked me in those letters because I left them in the tent. The tent isn't so far from here, but if I get up, I'll lose my chair. As I write this, at least ten other officers are standing around waiting for a place to sit. Yes, I'm in the "Officer's Club" again. It's tough here, but I hear it's tougher in France. Darling, I don't think I'll be able to send you a Christmas present this year. Just about all civilian goods are rationed over here except jewelry, and that is high priced and hard to get. Last night I saw some secret movies. War stuff. It's been raining most of the day, and I hope we move to decent quarters before snow flies (if we're here that long).

You are my everything, Gib

October 19, 1944, somewhere in France

My Dearest Wife, I'm in a little village in France with a bunch of other lieutenants as we wait for the rest of our outfit to catch up with us. When they arrive, we'll entrain for someplace else. Here we go. Now at the RR station. This is the first day I've been in Europe that it hasn't rained. The mud is terrific, just like the pictures you see in the newspapers. Last night, as the rain beat on our tent, I was thinking of the time you were down at my house before we were married. I was recuperating from my appendectomy. It was time for you to go home, and it was raining like mad and we dressed you in a lot of old clothes to keep you dry. You looked like a wet rag picker by the time I got you home. Continuing this three days later . . . I'm now at a replacement depot again somewhere in France. Must sign off.

I love you, Gib

October 19, 1944, somewhere in France

My Dearest Wife, now I'm sitting in a little village in France. I've just been talking with three little boys; Pierre, Jean and Georges. One of them reminded me of our little Kaaren. Like her, he was smart, good looking and full of the devil. I and a bunch of other lieutenants are waiting for the rest of our outfit to catch up to us before we entrain for someplace, I don't know where. But I am well and healthy and thinking of you all the time. Must sign off.

I love you, Gib

October 25, 1944, somewhere in France

My Darling, the town near us has a huge cathedral which looks beautiful from the outside, but I didn't have time to go in and chip souvenirs off the altar. Don't try to figure out where I am ... many cities in Europe have cathedrals. Something really amuses me about French cities. It's the public toilets in the streets. They are surrounded by a piece of sheet iron just tall enough to cover the gents from knee to chest. They can tip their hats to the ladies who pass by. I don't see myself using the things. Now I'm sitting in front of a hedge. Abercrombie is standing on my left. It looks like we're going to have a formation pretty soon. We're living in pup tents, and it's pretty primitive, but I'm in the same boat as a censored number of other officers, so I don't feel too bad. I haven't caught any colds, and as long as I have your love, I am happy.

Love from your lover, Gib

Later on, October 25, 1944, somewhere in France

Darling Genie ... Things can sure happen fast around here. Went to bed last night about 9:00 and at 10:30 was up again and had Abercrombie all packed up and shipped out. He was on orders to go to another replacement depot farther forward. So now I'm all alone in my little pup tent.

All my love, Gib

October 27, 1944, somewhere in France

Darling, I love you and miss you something awful. My morale is getting lower and lower all the time. Some letters from you would help a lot! I know you're writing, but I'm getting sent to so many locations and the mail can't catch up with me. Kiss Kaaren.

Love, Pop

October 28, somewhere in France

Dearest, I spent this morning cleaning and polishing my boots. Why I polished them is more than I can see since there's no place they can go around here that is free from mud. I had my bedding roll out on the ground airing a bit in the sunshine. Yes, actual sunshine. They showed a movie tonight: Kay Kyser in *Around the World*. They showed it out in a field, and we had to sit in the mud or stand up. I stood up. I had a peculiar dream last night. In the dream we spent the night at Pa's house, and in the morning I went into his room, and it was flooded with about three inches of water. That's all I remember. Must close now to get this in the afternoon mail. I love you.

You are my whole life, Gib

(I've always wondered if the dream about rising water might have something to do with Gib's growing realization of the proximity of danger.)

October 30, 1944, somewhere in France

My Darling, you'd die laughing if you could see me now. I'm sitting on a box out in front of my tent with a candle, holding the paper between my legs so I can see what I'm writing. Of course, I could have written all day but spent my time puttering and frittering. You know I'm good at that. Arranging stuff from one pile to another. Trying to get organized for when we're called forward. Don't get to town often, but today some of us got passes and went to see more of the cathedral. While we were in town, I bought some heavy underwear, and I found a tailor who helped me get a better fit on my old GI coat. Then we drank some wine in a nearby café. We caught a truck back to camp. It didn't have canvas on it And it was pouring rain. I thought for sure I'd catch pneumonia this morning, but so far, so good. I miss you so much. When I get home, I won't leave the house without you. It's only been a little over a month since I left, but it seems like years already. I still haven't had a letter from you since we left England. I'm all right, Darling. We had steak for supper tonight. The living conditions are primitive, but we do eat well, and that helps a lot. Now all I need is those back letters from you, and my morale will go way up. You're what I'm fighting this war for, and I want to come back to you when it's over.

Love from your ever-loving husband, Gib

November 1, 1944, Northwestern France

My Darling, this has been a beautiful day, just like those bright fall days at home – clear sunshine and a tang in the air. A good day to do my laundry. I had three one-gallon cans boiling on an open fire with my socks and underwear in them. I didn't get the stuff too clean, but I did get the caked mud off the socks and the smell out of the underwear. Oh, and I also got my handkerchiefs so I can stand to take them out of my pockets. I also aired my bedding, cleaned my weapons and just had a dandy time. Missed a chance to take a bath this afternoon. I had my stuff spread out all over the pasture and I couldn't get it collected in time to hop on the bus that was going to the field shower about four miles away. Darling, I didn't write yesterday, but I had plenty of time. It rained all day, and I stayed in bed in our tent most of the day, reading. I know I promised to write every day if I had time Well, I failed you yesterday. Sorry, Honey. I will try to do better. Next time you send me a package, will you please put in a bar of laundry soap?

Remember that I love you with all my heart, and I always will, Gib

November 6, somewhere in Belgium

My Darling, now I'm somewhere in Belgium. Our train on the way here went through Paris in the middle of the night, so we didn't get to see the city. We're living in a building that used to be either a hat factory or a laundry. I'm not sure which. It's the first building I've lived in since hitting England. This afternoon I went downtown to get some shoes repaired and see some of this place. It's a pretty big city, and I drank coffee in a café. I saw St. Nicholas in one of the stores. Children were waiting in line to let him know what they'd like for Christmas. That made me homesick because I imagine that's just what you're doing with Kaaren this year. I can't tell you any more tonight, Baby, except I love you.

I couldn't live without you, Gib

November 9, 1944, somewhere in Belgium

My Darling, my watch strap broke back in France and yesterday afternoon I got a chance to come downtown and have it replaced by a jeweler. I discovered after he had the new band on that he could not take French francs. I didn't have Belgian currency. But listen to this! Rather than take the strap back, he told me to come in when I had some Belgian francs and pay him then. I was so surprised at that I didn't know what to say. Time to get into my pup tent and go to bed. I have a new sleeping wardrobe now. I leave all my clothing on (except for my boots and helmet) and I use my GI coat as an additional blanket. When I get home, I'll have to get used to a bed gradually. First, I'll sleep on concrete, then on a wooden floor, then on a rug and gradually work my way up to a real bed.

I love you and think of you always, Gib

November 11, 1944, somewhere in Belgium

My Darling Wife, still in the same outfit, but now I live in a house instead of a factory. Moved across the street today, and now I'm in a small room right under the eaves on the third floor. Me and three other officers. We just sit here and wait for orders shipping us to forward battalions. The training program here seems to be just anything to keep the men busy and out of sight. I took a bunch of men out on a hike this morning. We went out of town, and sat on a hill for a while admiring the view, and marched back through town a bit and then back to the barracks. There's a perpetual poker game going on downstairs. It recesses for chow and bedtime. I'm not in the game because I don't know it, and I'd rather do a bit of reading. It's been doing a lot of raining, and it snowed on my birthday. I hope it freezes before I get up where the fighting is. I'd much rather fight on frozen ground than in the mud. I am fine, Baby.

I love you, Gib

(Knowing Gib's fondness for parades, I like to picture him marching around Brussels with his platoon of young privates. He has them in formation and shouts out their marching orders, bringing them to the Grand-Place in the city center, where they pass the Gothic City Hall and then on to St. Gulda's Cathedral.)

November 14, 1944, somewhere in Belgium

My Darling, yesterday I sent you a package. It's a perfume atomizer I found in a department store downtown. I hope you like it. I'm afraid it won't reach you by Christmas, but Merry Christmas a little late. I hope to God I'll be home next Christmas.

All my love and kisses to you and Kaaren, Gib

(The atomizer arrived shortly after Christmas and held a position of honor on my mother's dresser for years and years.)

November 17, 1944, somewhere in Germany

My Darling, someplace in Germany now. I'm still in the replacement system, no sign of being assigned to an outfit yet. Living in pyramidal tents here. No letters from you yet since I left England. As soon as I get to a division, all this mess will be straightened out because I'll have a permanent APO.

I love you always and more every day, Gib

November 18, 1944, Germany

Darling Baby, this isn't such a tough war so far. Yesterday and today, I've done nothing but play bridge, eat and sleep. We live in a big pyramidal tent with a stove and a round table in the middle, and we sit at the table reading and writing. Since I've been in this g__ d_____ replacement system, I've read *The Robe*, *Windswept*, *As the Earth Turns*, *The Last Adam*, a couple of Thorne Smith books and several mystery stories. We try to keep warm. I now have my bedding roll made up with four layers of blankets under me and three on top. With my GI overcoat on top of that, along with two folds of canvas, I manage to keep almost as warm as if I was at home, cuddled up beside you. There's an artillery outfit near us that makes a hell of a lotta racket but not quite enough to keep me awake at night. Buzz bombs go over now and then, and we all cross our fingers, hoping they'll pass us by. I haven't had a bath in a week, nor shaved for three days, but outside of that I'm all right. All that's wrong with me is that I want to come home to you and Kaaren. Your letters haven't caught up with me yet. They'll come any day soon, I hope.

All my love, Gib

(I'm enclosing twenty francs, Belgian currency.)

November 23, 1944, Hürtgen Forest, Germany: Gib's last letter

My Darling Genie, haven't much time to write, but at last I can send you my new address: Co E, 12th INF, APO, New York. It's on the envelope, but that may be mutilated. I'm O.K. and will continue to be so. Lots of wild things are said about battle troops, but the only disagreeable thing I've found so far is the living conditions. I love you, Darling, and think of you always. You're my plan for the post-war world.

All my love, Gib

(When I was older, my mother told me about the dream she'd had after the letters stopped coming. She saw someone like Gib in a dark forest. She could hear the noise of battle, smell gun smoke in the air and knew he'd come to say good-bye. Mom didn't tell anyone about her dream until later, but she made a note of it on a piece of her best stationery and tucked it into her top dresser drawer. It was dated November 30, 1944, the same day recorded in the telegram that came later reporting Gib's death. Further information from the War Office let our family know that Gib had been interred in the U.S. Military Cemetery #1, Henri-Chapelle, Belgium, Plot DD, and that the cemetery was under the constant care and supervision of United States Military Personnel. It wasn't until the fall of 1947 that Gib finally came home.

Thanks to the unimaginably difficult and logistically challenging work of The Graves Registration Service, he and about 6,200 of his fellow fallen soldiers aboard the Joseph V. Connolly were among the first of 170,000 to be repatriated from Europe. Gathered from their places of interment, carefully sealed into coffins made of bronze-toned steel and then placed in flag-covered shipping crates, they sailed from Antwerp and arrived in New York Harbor on October 26, 1947. The ship was decked in flowers and draped in mourning. An honor guard stood at attention. From there, the repatriated made their way to their hometowns or to national cemeteries.

Gib's flag-covered shipping crate arrived at the White-water train station, where family and friends had gathered. I was five at this time, deemed too young to go to the station. But I clearly remember being with everyone the next day as we sat in folding chairs in the sunshine at Hillside Cemetery. All our relatives from both sides of the family and all over Wisconsin and Minnesota walked silently up the hill to join us. I noticed that even the most affable and talkative aunts and uncles were strangely silent as they filled up the rows behind us. Everyone stood when a group of soldiers marched up the hill. They carried flags, guns and a bugle. Pastor Suby said a prayer. Colonel put his hand on my back just as three soldiers raised their guns to fire the salute. He'd told me that soldiers would be shooting guns and that it was okay to cover my ears but not to cry. The cemetery seemed extra quiet when the firing stopped. Two of the soldiers removed the flag from Gib's coffin, folded it in a special way and gave it to my mother. The coffin was lowered into the grave, and the bugler played "Taps." The soldiers marched away, and we all returned to our cars.

Colonel's green Olds led the way to the Congregational Church, where Lanny's friends had a meal ready for everyone. I don't remember exactly what was on the menu, but I'm pretty sure it consisted of creamed chicken, rice, peas and pumpkin pie. I remember that as we ate, my family found their voices again, and conversation ebbed and flowed. Several family friends told me that my mother and grandparents were lucky to have me because I was all they had left of Gib. I remember being unable to respond to them, and I've been pondering their words for the last 75 years, grateful for the honor but wary of its implications.)

Afterword

Gib's letters stopped coming, but Gib himself continued to be part of our lives. He smiled at us from photographs. His dog, Barbara, made the scene at every family function. His rowing machine remained available in my grandparents' attic in the house on Center Street. The perfume atomizer he sent from Brussels had a place of honor on my mother's dresser. Family and friends remembered his puns, his laugh, his practical jokes, his whimsy. And everyone reminded me how much I looked like him.

One day Lanny told me about Joe, the imaginary friend of Gib's childhood. Remembering that I was all that was left of Gib, I decided to have an imaginary friend, too. And just for good measure, I decided to have three imaginary friends: Henry, Joey and Smoky the horse. These three became a favorite topic of conversation at family gatherings. Lanny would ask me what Henry and Joey and Smoky had been doing, and I would invent bus trips to the Milwaukee Public Library, jaunts to Chicago to visit the aquarium, and fishing excursions on Lake Michigan, where their boat was swamped by the Loch Ness Monster. The wilder the tales, the better they went down. One evening, feeling unable to come up with new material, I amazed everyone (and myself) by announcing that Henry, Joey and Smoky had moved to Montana.

There were those who missed my imaginary friends, but I was happy they were now free to create their own adventures. No longer responsible for their comings and goings, I was able to fully enjoy taking summertime bike trips with friends to Cravath Lake or devouring chocolate-covered cones at the Dairy Queen. And on winter days, when Henry, Joey and Smoky were cross-country skiing in Montana, I met friends on top of the biggest hill in the park with my sled. When we weren't sledding, we were skating at the ice rink or sitting in the warming shed near the wood stove, drinking five-cent cups of hot chocolate. Occasionally, I wondered if Henry, Joey and Smokey were still enjoying Montana; I felt lucky to have had them around when I needed their company. My life was different when they went to Montana, but it was still a fine life.

The contours of my life altered even more significantly on an August day in 1956, when Mom married Clarence, a handsome and kind redhead who'd been a colleague of Gib's at the bank. With Mom's collaboration, he provided me with Pat, my redheaded sister, whose arrival brought the scent of baby powder to our house and prompted my friends to come around frequently to admire her cuteness and help me push her up and down Main Street in her blue-and-pink stroller. Pat has turned out to be a vast improvement over my imaginary friends. She would never decamp to an undisclosed location out West. She is a faithful constant in my life and a fun companion. She has flown to my side during illness and stayed until she was comfortable that I was well on the road to recovery. She has provided me with a brother-in-law who can fix anything, a lively and smart (and redheaded) niece and two charming and bright nephews.

When Pat went to kindergarten, I went to college, where I met Steve (now my husband). We've lived in Atlanta during most of our lives together. Our son, Andy, was born here. Mom and Clarence rushed to meet him during the first week of his life, and both said he reminded them of Gib. Mom said it was something about his eyes, and Clarence thought his voice sounded like Gib's. They were fond of him right away, just like Gib would have been if he'd had the opportunity to meet him. Our extended family made many trips south to see us, and we went north every Christmas and part of every July. Andy knows all his Wisconsin relatives and has spent fun times playing with his cousins there. They splashed in the lake in the summer and went sledding in the winter.

After graduating from Emory, Andy, now a writer like his grandfather, married the bright-eyed and musical Jenny. With her collaboration, they gave us two brilliant grandchildren, Hannah Ruth and Soren, who now live, along with Jenny's brother (our second son), Jason, in Savannah. We've visited that beautiful city so many times that we can give directions to the tourists. We've enjoyed school concerts, soccer games, graduations, birthday parties, Thanksgiving celebrations and beach weekends there.

Gib's letters sometimes come along on our trips to Savannah. We each pull one from the box and read it after supper. Hannah and Soren are familiar with Gib's story. They've stood outside his childhood home at 212 Center Street in Whitewater, Wisconsin. They've toured the bank where he used to work and visited his grave at Hillside Cemetery. They know about his imaginary friend, his dog, his practical jokes and his puns. They know Gib's letters are in the sturdy box upstairs in our house in Atlanta, where they can visit them any time they want to.

I too know they are there. They keep me tethered to everything important. They remind me of who I am and of the people who have loved and cared for me. Sometimes I imagine Gib lives up there in the attic. He wears a comfy robe and warm slippers. He reads, he looks out the window and he is always available for consultation. He has very few needs aside from knowing we are with him. I worry that life may be a bit dull up there for an extrovert like him. That's why I'm working to get his story, as told in his letters, out into the wider world. I'd hate to have him leave for Montana in hopes of finding adventure with other characters who have found their way West.

Addendum

The Family

Gib – Lt. Harold Gilbert Andersen, my father

Genie – Geneva Andersen, my mother, Gib's wife

Granny – Gib's mother, my grandmother, aka Lil, Ma, and
Lanny

Colonel – Gib's father, my grandfather, aka Harold Gilbert
Andersen Sr., Pa.

Uncle Jimmy – Gib's brother

Grammy – Genie's mother, my grandmother, aka Gertie

Barbara – Gib's Springer Spaniel who lived the rest of her
life with Genie's mother

Gib's Army Postings

Fort Sheridan, Chicago, December 1-5, 1942

Dec. 6-10, 1942 – Troop train to California

Camp Callan, San Diego, California, December 1942-March 6, 1943

March 7-9, 1942 – Troop train to North Carolina

Camp Davis, North Carolina, March 9, 1943-July 22, 1943, O.C.S. training

July 22 – August 2, 1943 – Furlough at home in Wisconsin

Camp Edwards, Massachusetts, August 5, 1943-December, 1943, (my mother and I join him from September to December)

Camp Davis, North Carolina, January 1, 1944-February 14, 1944

Fort Haan, Riverside, California, February 5-[date], 1944

Fort Hood, Killeen, Texas [date]-[date]

Censored location, somewhere in the Atlantic, September 14, 1944,

Censored location, somewhere in England, October 6, 1944-October 19, 1944

Somewhere in France, October 19, 1944-November 1, 1944

Somewhere in Belgium, November 6, 1944-November 14, 1944

Somewhere in Germany, November 17, 1944-November 30, 1944

Hürtgen Forest, November 30, 1944, Gib killed in action, Aachen, Germany; interred in U.S. Military Cemetery #1, Henri-Chapelle, Belgium, Plot DD

Fall 1947, Gib repatriated home to Whitewater, Wisconsin